The LOVE LIES

10 Revelations That Will TRANSFORM YOUR RELATIONSHIPS and ENRICH YOUR LOVE LIFE

Dear Deborah —
The Love Truths
Shall make you
free! In-Joy,
Debrena J. Gandy

The LOVE LIES

**10 Revelations That Will
TRANSFORM YOUR RELATIONSHIPS
and ENRICH YOUR LOVE LIFE**

DEBRENA JACKSON GANDY
FOREWORD BY ACTRESS KIM COLES

SUNRISE
River Press

SUNRISE
River Press

Sunrise River Press
39966 Grand Avenue
North Branch, MN 55056
Phone: 651-277-1400 or 800-895-4585
Fax: 651-277-1203
www.sunriseriverpress.com

Edit by Allyson E. Machate
Layout by Monica Seiberlich

ISBN 978-1-934716-54-0
Item No. SRP654

Library of Congress Cataloging-in-Publication Data

Gandy, Debrena Jackson.
 The love lies : 10 revelations that will transform your relationships and enrich your love life / by Debrena Jackson Gandy.
     pages cm
 ISBN 978-1-934716-54-0
 1. Man-woman relationships. 2. Love. 3. Common fallacies. I. Title.
 HQ801.G297 2014
 306.7–dc23
 2014006520

Printed in USA
10 9 8 7 6 5 4 3 2 1

Dedication

To Joe, my sexy and amazing husband, partner, lover,
and man of my dreams.

To my beautiful and brilliant daughters, Adera, Kiana, and Kenzie,
who constantly inspire me to model being a deeply satisfied and fulfilled woman, wife, and mother.

To Nathaniel and Thelma Jackson, my incredible and dynamic parents—I thank God for choosing to bring me into this world through
the two of you.

To Ericka, my sister—one of the most beautiful, brilliant,
and savvy women that I know.

To Nathaniel, my brother, and one of the "quickest wits" on the planet,
and to Kalii, my beautiful and brilliant niece.

To the Love Academy host and co-hosts across the country and the
hundreds of Love Academy and Men-tality participants from coast to
coast who believed in this work and who were the *first* to say YES to
being a part of the Relationships Revolution.

Contents

Foreword

by Kim Coles

When I met Debrena, I immediately knew that I had met a kindred spirit. I was introduced to her by her brother, a fellow comic when I was performing in Seattle a while ago. Her energy was contagious, her smile lit up the room, and she exuded grace and fabulosity! We reconnected a few weeks later and went on to have a great time collaborating on a successful inspirational on-line project together.

One of the things I love about Debrena is that she is the "real deal." She's authentic and transparent. As she takes you on this journey, she shares candidly from her own life. She doesn't claim to be an expert, but she is a messenger of 10 revelations about love relationships that "change the game."

As I reflect over my relationships, I can see that when I wasn't clear about my worth, value, and self-esteem, I had disastrously unhealthy relationships. (Love relationships sure have a way of being a ruthless barometer of where we *really* are in our self-esteem.) So I attracted confused men, or confusing signals *from* men.

I also had that looooong What-I-Want-in-a-Man List, but couldn't figure out why the men I dated were what I *didn't* want in a man. I was caught up in a line of thinking about relationships and about men and myself that was typical, and a function of my social conditioning. I didn't question what I'd come to accept as true and I couldn't understand why in this area of my life, things were out of alignment, and not consistent with the success I was experiencing in my professional life.

If *The Love Lies* had been available to me back then, I would have seen the light. Hallelujah! I would have been able to recognize the Love Lies in my beliefs and interactions with men. I would have seen the Love Lies alive and well in my "hunt and seek" mission to "find" The One/Mr. Right, even though Mr. Wrong kept showing up. I would have seen them in the futile search outside of myself for love and in my belief that a man could "complete me" or "make me happy."

Now, all in one book, the toxic beliefs are revealed so that we can replace them with the Love Truths and, most important, "detox" and heal ourselves. *The Love Lies* gets to the *root* cause of our relationship struggles and dysfunction.

Juicy love relationships are what Debrena calls "rare air." Now that I've done the "self work," and learned to be honest with myself, I understand what intimacy really means. As I've learned to love and value myself, I've continued to attract a higher quality of men. I am now experiencing an amazing love relationship with a wonderful man, and it is indeed, "rare air."

When I read *The Love Lies*, I knew that it was going to be the start of a Relationships Revolution, or more accurately, a Relationships *Evolution* for you and for me!

Get ready... this is more than a book—it is a Movement!

Laughter and Love,

Kim Coles

Acknowledgments

For me, writing a book is akin to birthing a baby. Like a baby, a new book is a creation that goes through a gestation period, develops in the creative womb, has a due date, and even has a "birthing team." This book, especially, will always hold a special place in my heart because it had a 13-year gestation period!

Overflowing gratitude to my literary agent extraordinaire, Linda Konner, who was this "book baby's" #1 advocate.

Kissing your feet with humble and profound thanks to my book proposal editor, Michele Brown, who was instrumental in helping me put into words what was in my heart.

Boundless thanks to my publisher, Molly Koecher, who is progressive in her thinking and her life outlook, and "got" this book and its message right from the start.

Kudos to the team at Sunrise River Press for being downright amazing (Connie I LOVE the cover design; Zac, thanks for masterminding the online strategy), and embracing the vision for this book.

Endless hugs and kisses to my editor, Ally Machate, who was this book baby's spiritual midwife and "birthing coach," and to Redessa Harris, my publicist, who "caught the vision" and helped me share it with the world.

A victorious "high five" to this book's spiritual "godmothers," Jolyn Gardner Campbell, Karimah Stewart, Cammie Clinton, Stephanie Jordan, Delayna Elliott, Deborah Nelons, Ericka Jackson, Dr. Thelma Jackson, Jacqueline Nash, Tamara Lumpkin, Angela Mack, Jada Pettigrew, Fralisa McFall, Erin Anthony, and Patrice Sidoione, for believing in this book and never letting go of the vision for it.

Endless gratitude to my readers, attendees, students, mentees, and participants over the years who have continued to read my books, attend my events, keynotes, and retreats, purchase my products and programs, and take my courses and tele-seminars, year after year.

Abundant appreciation to the Inner Circle, my sacred group of best friends who are my prayer warriors and the wind beneath my wings. You know who you are.

An expansive "Thank You!" to Team Debrena, the amazing women and men who are part of my incredible marketing, website, and promotion team.

And an eternal thank you, Holy Spirit, for graciously guiding me through every step of this transformational process and for the privilege of receiving and sharing these relationship revelations with the world.

A Special Note to You from Me

Dear Reader,

As I reflect over the past 13 years of my life, surprisingly, the number of years that has lapsed since the release of my last nationally published book, my heart is filled with gratitude. My initial plan was to have certainly released a third book within a few years of my second book. I never anticipated, however, that well over a decade would lapse between book #2, *All the Joy You Can Stand*, and book #3—but here we are. And oh, what a journey it's been!

I now know that this 13-year lapse of time was necessary and purposeful, instead of a seeming delay. It allowed me to move through an important spiritual rite of passage within myself and within my relationship, one that set the stage for this book. Inside this 13-year lapse of time, I experienced what was the darkest and most challenging season of my life, thus far. I was literally brought to my knees by the deterioration and subsequent breakdown of my marriage in year ten. After four years of doing all we knew how to do to try and "save" our marriage, including seeking both professional and spiritual help, both my husband and I were emotionally exhausted, and ready to call it quits. It was while in the midst of this crisis that I received a series of divinely inspired "spiritual downloads" about love relationships. Acting on these downloads changed my life.

My husband and I went from teetering on the brink of divorce to a marriage that has been renewed and transformed. From that moment to now has been nothing less than remarkable. Quite frankly, it's been miraculous. This book is about the insights I received that I both heard and heeded, that enabled our relationship to experience a transformational turn-around.

As a result, we've been able to move beyond having a happy marriage, to having one that is *juicy*, deeply satisfying, and fulfilling, and better than *ever*! I'm very clear that this is "rare air." This book reveals the profound insights that brought us "from brink to breakthrough," and from "teetering to transformed," revelations that can be applied to your current or future relationship(s), whether you are single, married, engaged, or divorced.

Why I Wrote this Book

I wrote this book, first and foremost, because I was divinely guided to chronicle a powerful journey and process. I wrote it to share a set of mind-blowing, or better yet, belief-blowing insights I received during the lowest point and darkest hour in my relationship—counter-intuitive insights that led to transformation, first in myself, and subsequently, a remarkable restoration and transformation in my marriage.

Second, I wrote this book to be a wake-up call that introduces you to a set of new, liberating ways of believing, thinking, and engaging in your relationships that have not been presented in quite this way anywhere else.

Third, this book is to serve as a shovel to help us dig up what is at the root of our typical yet failing approach to relationships—one that yields far too much frustration, irritation, hurt, pain, confusion, dysfunction, and disappointment.

Fourth, it is to serve as a bullhorn so that we can boldly call out the deeply flawed beliefs and thus the insanity we've been experiencing in our love relationships for far too long.

Fifth, it is to serve as a balm that heals and "detoxes" us of the Love Lies, and breaks us free from the poisonous, damaging and, for some, even deadly effects of our current approach to relationships.

And last, it is to serve as a flashlight, to help illuminate the truths that are the path to a *new* model of relationships—one that supports self-expression and deep satisfaction and fulfillment for both women and men.

It is no accident that you and this book have found each other. It is a divine appointment.

The concept for *The Love Lies* was born out of the success and popularity of the live Love Academy intensives for women and the Men-tality seminars for men I first started leading around the country a few years ago. These live courses, based upon the sharing of the first few of these divinely inspired insights, continue to this day. I was touched and moved by the testimonies that poured in about the powerful outcomes experienced by participants in my Love Academy intensives, courses, and seminars who took the teachings and principles to heart and applied them in their lives and relationships. The feedback from participants confirmed that a book would be a fitting medium for taking this message to a wider audience. It is my hope that the insights shared here will impact you profoundly as they did in my life and relationship and in the lives and relationships of hundreds upon hundreds of others across the country.

On a warm summer night a few months ago, I sat with a girlfriend enjoying a delicious dinner and glass of wine on the patio of one of our favorite restaurants. We were reminiscing about the terrain that had been covered on my journey from my marriage breakdown and breakthrough to the inception of this book. To acknowledge and celebrate this milestone, she summed it up perfectly when she held up her wine glass with a huge smile on her face and made a toast: *"Cheers! Here's to the start of a relationships revolution!"*

So here's to the start of a relationships revolution, and to you becoming a fellow Relationships Revolutionary! Cheers!

With Gratitude,

Debrena

Debrena Jackson Gandy

Part 1

Laying the Foundation

Introduction

WARNING!
This book could be hazardous to
the insane love relationships beliefs
you've come to hold as true.

WHAT IF . . . we have been socially conditioned into ways of believing, thinking, behaving, and relating that are inherently flawed and continually set us up for relationships failure?

WHAT IF . . . these beliefs create a relationships model that makes achieving and *sustaining* deep satisfaction and fulfillment virtually impossible?

WHAT IF . . . our male/female relationship conflicts and problems persist because we have been addressing the effects and symptoms but not the underlying beliefs that are the root of the problems?

Scientist Albert Einstein is noted as describing insanity as doing the same thing over and over again, yet expecting different results. And insanity is what has characterized the Western approach to relationships for decades and even centuries. *The Love Lies* reveals how each of the above what-if statements is true and exposes the faulty, toxic beliefs—the "Love Lies"—that are the underlying culprits.

Drinking from a Poisonous Well

Several months ago I was having a conversation with an East Coast client who flew to Seattle to have a private relationships coaching weekend with me. As we sat at the kitchen table at my mentor's retreat home having one of our sessions, I described the prevailing insanity in our male/female relationships using a metaphor. I explained, "It's like continuing to repeatedly lower a bucket into a water well, retrieving the water, and then handing out cups of water to others to drink when we have clear evidence that the water is poisonous: people are bent over, nauseous, vomiting, and clenching their stomachs, yet we lower the bucket again and again, insisting on passing out water even though people continue to get sicker and sicker." This pattern is hauntingly familiar in our approach to relationships. Clearly the basic premises, and foundational beliefs from which we've been operating, are similarly tainted. You could say that we're suffering from an epidemic of "Love STDs." In this case, I mean "socially transmitted delusions" about love relationships, instead of sexually transmitted diseases.

The relationship approach we have been using has failed the majority of us miserably—it is flawed and dysfunctional *by design*. The evidence is compelling and undeniable; yet the insanity causes us to recycle and repackage the same old Love Lies repeatedly. Too often, the poisoning is aided and abetted by talk shows, magazine articles, music lyrics, TV shows, and movies.

The fallout from these Love STDs has taken a great toll on both women and men. For women, the toll has taken the form of crippled self-confidence, deep distrust, eroded self-worth, dependency, loneliness, rage, depression, misuse or abuse of our bodies, sexual promiscuity, pessimism, hopelessness, regret, shame, jealousy, and even broken or damaged female friendships. Even physical diseases can, over time, manifest from thought patterns and behaviors riddled with the Love Lies, especially degenerative diseases such as breast, cervical, or uterine cancer; uterine fibroids, cysts, or tumors; and even obesity and high blood pressure, to name a few.

For men the results are equally devastating: They suffer from pressure to perform and provide; feelings of inadequacy for not measuring up to what feels like impossible expectations; feelings of emasculation; the perception that much of the behavior exhibited by females in relationships is downright crazy; using sex as a substitute for the risk of emotional connection and/or using sex as an escape or a physical or stress relief; or passivity. Not to mention physical diseases such as prostate cancer, heart disease, heart attack, and lung cancer.

In recent years I've been delighted to see new books that look at our country's relationship challenges through a more spiritual lens. In this book you may encounter some Love Lies that seem familiar at first glance, especially if you've been a student of personal growth and spiritual development. For example, it is likely that you've encountered books that discuss the importance of loving yourself first, before trying to love another. But we may be unaware of the underlying female Love Lies that can make self-love a struggle

[handwritten margin note:] Preparation for covenant marriage is not just about me & my life. It is also good for social & public health.

for us in the first place. Or we may have read books that provide tips on how to "select and reject" when out on a date, but we may not be aware of how the Love Lies negatively impact our very perception of what dating is and how it works. We may be unaware that the very context of modern dating is based upon faulty premises and false claims that then go on to set the stage for our high rate of break-ups and divorces.

Referring back to the water well analogy, *The Love Lies* reveals what is making the water poisonous in the first place—a specific set of toxic underlying beliefs, the Love Lies, that have been infecting our thinking and thus poisoning our relationships. *The Love Lies* departs from the usual approach to relationship problems that puts the focus on the *effects* of our dysfunction, and instead exposes and addresses the underlying causes so that we can detox and heal, putting an end to the insanity once and for all.

Where My Journey Began:
From Relationship Breakdown to Breakthrough

After 10 years of what would be considered a happy marriage and certainly what would be considered a very decent marriage by most, my marriage experienced a crippling breakdown and entered a tailspin that caused it to nearly crash and burn. After four years of trying to save our marriage, it looked like the only option remaining was to move forward with divorce proceedings. By year 14 of our marriage, my husband and I both wanted out.

So what occurred between the celebrated day we got married—in an elaborate wedding with nearly 500 guests that was featured in an issue of *Glamour* magazine—and the day my husband and I sat down in the office of a divorce attorney to begin discussing divorce? The short answer: *a lot*.

In the 10th year of our marriage, it came to light that my husband and I had *both* been engaged in multiple sexual affairs, over a span of several years. We were both engaged in what I now call serial infidelity. Whew! It's enough of a challenge to deal with one partner cheating with one person, but both of us, over time, with different individuals?

It's certainly not easy to announce something like this to the world in the pages of a book, but it is a real part of our journey. I'm leveling with you about this, up front, and you can count on me to continue to be transparent with you throughout this book. I now realize that having the uncommon experience of being on both ends of infidelity—as a violator and betrayer, as well as a "violatee" and "betrayee"—has given me greater understanding and deeper insights into the often subtle but consistent types of dynamics that open doors and contribute to a relationship becoming vulnerable to infidelity.

After this shattering realization it certainly would have been much easier to throw in the towel and get divorced. But instead we tried talking it out. We tried counseling with one counselor, then with a second counselor, with our pastor at the time, and then a second pastor, and then a therapist. We tried talking it out again and again. We'd seem to make a few steps of progress, then one of us would get triggered or old "stuff" would resurface and we would regress and backslide several steps.

The road to reconciliation seemed too slippery and steep. The emotional gunk, funk, and junk that had built up between us felt like Mt. Everest—a mountain too high to climb.

My turning point

One day shortly after our first meeting with a divorce attorney, I was doing my morning prayer and meditation. While sitting there on my bedroom floor, frustrated and teary-eyed, I admitted to God that I was at the end of my rope. I was out of strategies, techniques, and new approaches. I was exhausted and ready to throw in the towel. "*What do you want me to do now?!*" I asked, as I cried out to God in both anger and exasperation.

God's simple reply to me was: Thanks for finally asking.

It was then that God presented me with an invitation.

He invited me to enter into a process in which He would not only restore, but completely transform, our marriage. As a result of going through this process, my marriage was going to be better than ever, He promised. It was going to be the manifestation of the extraordinary and deeply satisfying and fulfilling marriage I had journaled about as far back as my high school diary-with-the-locket days. When He mentioned what I'd written in my high school diary 25 years earlier, I almost fell over with surprise. I had long-forgotten what I'd written in those diary pages, but apparently God hadn't. He let me know that He was going to reveal powerful insights to me that would enable me to be a catalyst and an agent of change in birthing a new, transformed marriage out of what was a dying relationship.

Oh, but there was a caveat: He assured me that He would direct me and guide me every step of the way, but I had to follow His guidance and instruction without deviation. He assured me that as a result of my obedience I would be given powerful insights and truths that would benefit not only me and my husband but many, many other people as well—both single and married.

Even after all of this, I *still* hesitated. After four years of trying to save our marriage under my belt, I was both skeptical and resigned. Most of all, I was emotionally worn out. So instead of immediately jumping at this invitation, I thought to myself: What is going to be so new or different that I haven't already tried? After mulling this proposition over in my mind for the next 30 minutes, I asked, "God, so are you *sure* that me saying yes to this invitation and following your lead is going to help a lot of other people?"

God's answer was an unequivocal "yes."

So, in that pivotal moment, I let out a big sigh and decided that my answer would be "yes." My marriage became destined for a different trajectory in that moment. It was a decision that was to become a critical turning point. This *yes* was to change me, my marriage, and my life—forever. Little did I know at the time that I was going to be introduced to a new model for relationships that would later become the basis for my Love Academy intensives and seminars and, eventually, this book. To this day I continue to be amazed at how lives and relationships of both single and married women and men around the country are being transformed by applying these principles and teachings.

Over the next 90 days I received a series of what I can best describe as "divine downloads" that came *through* me, not *from* me. These spiritual downloads consisted of a specific set of severely flawed and faulty beliefs that undergirded our prevailing approach to relationships and perpetuated the familiar yet warped Western cultural understanding of love relationships. Nearly every other day I received another download until I had a total of 50 Love Lies that clearly were along gender lines, 25 specific to women and 25 specific to men. They blew my mind. As I reviewed this final list of flawed relationship beliefs, I exclaimed, "These are a bunch of *lies!*" Hence, the origin of the name *The Love Lies*. It is the first 10 of the revelations specific to women, the female Love Lies, that I share in this book.

At that time I had two best-selling books under my belt, and I'd been designing and leading personal growth and spiritual development events and courses for nearly 15 years. I considered myself rather evolved (*evolved*, said with a high-browed British accent), so I was stunned to discover, and so was my ego, that my beliefs, thinking, actions, reactions, emotions, and behaviors were riddled with the Love Lies. No, not *me*, I initially thought. It was hard to acknowledge, at first, the degree to which the Love Lies were embedded in nearly every aspect of my relationships life. The process I entered into forced me to recognize the corresponding patterns of thinking, behaving, and communicating the Love Lies spawned; and finally, release and replace the Love Lies with the Love Truths through what I termed my "detox" process.

I had to 'fess up and begin to tell the truth to myself about myself. As each additional Love Lie was unearthed, I was able to recognize its manifestations and symptoms, and pull it out by the root. This process started with me and then rippled outward to my husband and then our marriage. Over the next two years we were able to, against all odds, experience a complete relationship turnaround. What began with my personal healing and transformation became the catalyst for the healing and transformation of my marriage.

Beginning in 2009, I first started sharing a few of the downloads during a monthly tele-seminar that attracted women and men from across the country. It soon evolved into me piloting a seminar in my living room with eight friends, that then progressed into the birth of a live full-day course that I called the "Love Academy."

Since that first informal for-women-only intensive in my living room, the Love Academy teachings and principles have touched and impacted the lives of hundreds of female participants, and even eventually expanded to include live for-men-only "Men-tality" seminars.

Have You "Bought" the Love Lies?

When you are operating from one or more of the female Love Lies, there are definite clues and cues. The Love Lies leave a clear trail of fingerprints. When the Love Lies have taken root in your beliefs and thinking, and thus your emotions and behaviors, then either consciously or unconsciously, you tend to

- speak of looking for or trying to find The One or Mr. Right;
- have trouble sustaining healthy and fulfilling relationships;
- make statements that reference "lowering your standards" or "having to settle" when talking about men;
- experience poor, disrespectful, or insensitive treatment from men;
- believe you can't change a man;
- have a What-I-Want-in-a-Man or a What-I'm-Looking-for-in-a-Man list;

- repeatedly hear from men that you're "too independent," "high maintenance," or intimidating;
- experience a pattern of men saying they're going to call, especially after a first date, and they don't;
- feel continually disappointed by men;
- often feel frustrated or irritated in your relationship(s);
- open your legs too soon to sex or your relationships with men quickly become sex-centered or sex-dependent;
- often feel uncertain about "where things are going" in your relationship(s);
- have the expectation that a man is supposed to "make you happy" or "meet your needs";
- feel that you are communicating clearly in your relationship though you're not seeing the desired change in behavior or getting the response that you'd like;
- find yourself deferring certain life experiences or adventures, and putting your life on hold, until you've met The One or gotten married;
- find yourself "waiting on the Lord" to send you a husband yet you're not actively engaged in preparing your mind, body, spirit, or finances;
- feel like you're the one carrying most of the "load" in your relationship(s);
- focus on the kid/kids, if married with kid/kids; or you
- find yourself nagging and complaining a lot about your husband or to him, if married.

How many of these apply to you? These may seem like typical or familiar tendencies whether you're single or married, and ones that are echoed by many other females you see, hear, or observe around you and in the media. However, it's important to realize that these types of patterns of thinking, behaving, and interacting in our relationships are actually some of the classic by-products of the Love Lies. If any of these apply to you, you're not alone.

Who is affected by the Love Lies?

There are seven distinguishing characteristics of those most affected, or shall we say, infected, by the female Love Lies. As you read through the characteristics, you'll notice the specific segment of females that is most affected, though not exclusively.

- The Love Lies are "installed" through "Western-American" forms of social conditioning—modes and methods undergirded by the converging ideologies of individualism, capitalism, and materialism.
- In general, the Love Lies are most present in females acculturated and socialized in the Western/American culture, regardless of ethnicity. My research shows, based upon representative samplings from Love Academy participants, there's an 85 percent or greater chance you're operating from five or more of the Love Lies if you were raised and acculturated in the United States.
- The Love Lies are more likely to apply to females born between the years 1950 and 1986. (Please note that I said *more likely to apply*, not that they *only* apply to females born within this birth year range.) Thus the Love Lies tend to apply especially across the span of three particular generations: Baby Boomers, Generation Xers, and some of the older Generation Y/Millennials.
- The female Love Lies can transcend age, generation, ethnicity, nationality, and even religion.
- The Love Lies can transcend your relationship status and can be in effect whether you are single, married, or divorced.
- The Love Lies apply within the domain of male-female relationships specifically.
- In this domain, 90 percent or more of us are operating "in our girl"—an immature level of emotional, spiritual, and "communicational" development.

Instead of being directed toward single women or married women, this book is for both. Unless you were already detoxed, if you are or were married, then you brought the Love Lies into your marriage with you. If you are single, and this includes those who are now divorced, this book's teachings, principles, and practices can prepare you for your next or a new relationship. If you are currently married and experiencing cycles of complacency, disappointment, frustration, or irritation, or these have become the norm, then these teachings, principles, and practices can provide a platform for transforming you and your marriage. If you are currently married and you consider your marriage "good," then this book will help you take it from good to great, or from great to amazing.

Information Doesn't Equal Transformation

Have you noticed? Ingesting information is not the same as experiencing transformation. This book can truly be transformational for you if you are willing to engage in the inner spiritual, mental, and emotional self-work that is required in order to experience profound change within. When you transform within, it always becomes apparent without. Transformation, by design, requires the courage to truthfully look at yourself in the mirror, then examine, challenge, and replace long-standing ways of thinking, choosing, and behaving that aren't working for you. Finally, you must actually receive, act on, and apply these teachings and principles.

Amazon.com lists more than 37,000 books (yes, 37,000!) on the topics of relationships and marriage alone. Then we have thousands of marriage and relationship counselors nationwide, more than a hundred blog sites, hundreds of magazine articles, and numerous TV talk–show and reality-show experts that address relationships. So the issue is *not* a shortage of information—we actually have an avalanche of relationships information available to us—but the quantity of information has not translated into transformation or deep and profound inner and outer change.

Too often relationships advice is shallow, confusing, or conflicting. This misleads us into thinking that achieving and sustaining deeply satisfying and fulfilling relationships consists merely of adhering to a set of numbered how-to action steps and techniques. The preponderance of information tends to address only external, visible problems or behaviors without exploring the underlying beliefs, and thus has us applying, retrying, and re-applying this how-to advice without real success or lasting results. When things go wrong, we think we've simply missed a step, or that we need to move on to what we think is a better formula.

Clearly, something is gravely and fundamentally wrong in how we've been trying to address our myriad problems. The evidence is daunting. The United States boasts the highest *worldwide* divorce rate, one that has increased in recent years to nearly 51 percent. According to the annual report on marriage published by the National Marriage Project, when we "give it another try," we don't fare better. As a matter of fact, the failure rate climbs! The majority of second marriages (60 percent) and third marriages (73 percent) end in divorce in this country. These percentages are a powerful indictment of a flawed understanding of love and an approach to relationships and marriage that consistently produces a high rate of failure.

With such a shockingly high divorce rate, cohabitating may seem to be a strategy for avoiding future marital discord or divorce, but the National Survey of Families and Households found that couples who cohabitate before marriage are actually 50 percent *more* likely to divorce. Author and relationship expert Nancy Pina makes a powerful observation with which I concur. She writes, "living together is not divorce prevention, nor does it seem to be marriage preparation."

One might argue that the problem lies in the choices we make for our relationship partners in the first place, and not how we approach relationships themselves. However, *Online Dating Magazine* estimates that there are now more than 500 dating sites, and yet, according to research published in the *Proceedings of the National Academy of Science*, the access to a larger selection of possible partners online has not translated into higher levels of relationship satisfaction. To the contrary, online dating has created a whole new host of frustrations and obstacles, for many.

In fact, levels of satisfaction have continued to slowly and steadily decline over the past 35 years among couples who consider their marriages "very happy," from an average of 67.5 percent "very happy" down to 61.5 percent, for both males and females. Furthering the cause for concern are several studies showing that marital satisfaction is at its peak when a couple first marries, experiences a consistent decline in satisfaction over time, and drops to its lowest when the first child is a teenager. These are very sobering facts.

The big picture

When we look at the big picture, there are clues to why we struggle so greatly with sustaining successful relationships and marriages in this country. Interestingly, research shows that divorce rates vary drastically on a global level, depending on whether a country identifies as "individualist" versus "collectivist." A study conducted on 26 nations by social psychologist Geert Hofstede compared a country's degree of individualism or collectivism, and discovered that there was a direct correlation between individualism or collectivism orientation and divorce rates: the more individualistic a country, the higher its divorce rate. And worldwide, guess which country ranks as the most individualistic? The United States. It follows that we also have the highest divorce rate of any country on the planet! Let's take a look for a moment at the divorce rates in other individualistic countries to see how they stack up. Compared to the 51 percent divorce rate in the United States, the divorce rate in the United

Kingdom (number two in the study), is approximately 32 percent, and 25 percent in Canada (ranking at number three in individualism). In contrast, the divorce rates in collectivistic countries are dramatically lower. For example, Jamaica's divorce rate is 4 percent, Mexico's is 3.4 percent, Italy's is 2.8 percent, and Brazil's is 2.7 percent.

By definition, people in individualistic or Western societies, such as the United States, Canada, and countries in Western Europe, value self-interest and the pursuit of personal goals above the interests or well-being of society or one's community. This can be summed up as the "I mentality." Individualistic countries also tend to put a high emphasis on personal independence, personal achievement, looking out for oneself or only immediate family members, self-reliance, and making decisions based upon individual needs. Collectivistic countries, on the other hand, value group interest and community welfare over self-interest, and see themselves as members of a larger society or community where interests of the group come first. This can be summed up as the "We mentality."

I realize that this data does not take into consideration every possible related variable, such as level of divorce tolerance due to religious beliefs; nonetheless, the implications are compelling.

A clash of titans

The "I mentality" leads to being overly self-centered and self-focused and seems to have diminished our capacity for giving, sharing, open-heartedness, and expressing authentic care and concern for another and warped our understanding of love—all of which are essential in healthy love relationships. In addition to individualism, our warped understanding of love is supported by two other major Western-American culture titans: materialism and capitalism. Our culture's bias toward a material-based interpretation of reality has bled over to taint our understanding of love. We've been attempting to interpret love through a filter of materialism. Materialism values tangible, material objects—physical possessions, creature comforts, and the "seen" three-dimensional world—over inner qualities, spiritual values, well-being, inner peace, joy, and the "unseen" spiritual world. Yet love is first a spiritual phenomenon—a living force and a living energy that is unseen yet real.

Capitalism, our country's economic philosophy, is based on the notion of scarcity—there's not enough "supply" to go around. The production and distribution of goods and services is privately controlled, and the goal is to make profits. Thus, in much the same way that we might chase or pursue the "almighty dollar," we exhibit similar chase-and-pursue scarcity behavior in relationships.

We perceive, approach, and experience relationships through a lens tainted by the above-mentioned "isms," and consequently, separate them from their inherent spiritual reality. To add insult to injury, the behaviors that are fed by these isms, are fraught with ego, conditionality, and selfishness, all of which run counter to love. These isms combine to obviously handicap and diminish our capacity to understand, attract, and *sustain* juicy, deeply satisfying love relationships.

Yes, Western cultures may excel in business, economics, industry, and technology, but clearly *not* in the area of relationships. We have an epidemic of more relationship failure than success. I assert that our individualistic culture, combined with our ideologies of materialism and capitalism, amplify challenges and exacerbate frustrations and conflicts when it comes to our love relationships.

A Brief Overview of the First 10 Female Love Lies

As I mentioned earlier, I "received" a total of 25 female Love Lies and 25 male Love Lies. Trying to cover them all would be too overwhelming for one book; instead, in this book we're focusing on the first 10 female Love Lies, the 10 that are the most foundational.

Love Lie #1: Love Is Found
This is the biggest Love Lie, the one that has us treat love as a "thing" to look for, try to find, or to acquire from another in a love relationship. It reflects our fundamentally warped understanding of what love really is.

Love Lie #2: A Man Completes Me
This Love Lie has us seek completion through a male, has us look to a man to fill voids within us, and even has us putting certain aspects of our lives on hold until we "find" the one who is supposed to "make" us happy.

Love Lie #3: I Have a Sole Soul Mate
Based in scarcity, this Lie has us believe that there is only one solitary, designated man on the planet with whom we have the possibility of developing, achieving, or experiencing a soul-level connection.

Love Lie #4: Self-Love Is Optional
This Lie tricks us into believing that damaged self-esteem, low self-worth, self-condemnation, and guilt can be ignored and disregarded and have no significant bearing on our ability to give and receive love, and attract and sustain healthy relationships.

Love Lie #5: My "Requirements List" Ensures that I Find "The One"
This Lie has us give more power to a descriptive shopping list of features and requirements of what we want in The One, than to cultivating within ourselves the attitude, qualities, and ways of being that naturally draw healthy love to us.

Love Lie #6: Having Expectations Ensures I "Get" What I Want from a Man
This Love Lie convinces us that a fulfilling relationship is the result of getting our needs met. We believe that having a prescribed list of supposed-to-, ought-to-, and should-based expectations is the key to getting what you want from a man.

Love Lie #7: Dating Is How I Really Get to Know a Man
Dating, as we now know it and do it, has become a fast-paced, sort-and-reject process of elimination through which we judge and assess superficial facts on an internal "scorecard," all while claiming that our intent is to "really get to know him."

Love Lie #8: He Should Already Know
The He-Should-Already-Know Syndrome has us believe that a man should already know certain things that we consider important—namely, our desires and preferences, our dislikes, what we're thinking, and what we want him to do in any given moment or situation. We expect a man to come preloaded with these "knowings."

Love Lie #9: I Can't Change a Man
This is often stated like a truism, especially by talk-show experts, though it is based in the false belief that a man is fixed, static, and unchanging in a relationship. This Lie has us believe "that's just the way he is," or "that's just the way men are." Since nagging and complaining hasn't worked successfully, we mistakenly conclude that "you can't change a man."

Love Lie #10: I Am the Follower
Regardless of how it may appear, a male's behavior is in response to cues received from the female, whether verbal or nonverbal, subtle or overt, and whether she's aware of this dynamic or not. This Lie reveals that we don't recognize that, in fact, females are leading the interactions with men by setting the pace, tone, and quality of the interactions. This applies in marriage also.

Female vs. woman

A little heads up before we go any further. Going forward in this book, you'll notice I frequently use the term "female" instead of "woman." This is on purpose. Woman is not a term I use loosely.

In this book, *woman* is a sacred designation that represents not just reaching a certain biological age, but more important, being evolved in your ways of thinking, being, behaving, responding, and relating; and also being mature emotionally, spiritually, mentally, and "communicationally." When we get to the chapter on making the shift from being "in your girl" to being "in your woman," you'll have the opportunity to complete a personal assessment to see exactly where you stand in this girl-woman continuum. I'll also share with you specific ways to make this all-important shift. I've found, however, that until we make this shift, experiencing deep satisfaction and fulfillment in relationships will be elusive. Making this shift from girl to woman also is a powerful indicator that you're truly letting go of the Love Lies and, more and more, embracing the Love Truths.

Now it's time to more deeply explore the underlying source of the problems endemic to our current relationships paradigm, the Love Lies, and set ourselves free.

Chapter One

Preparing for the Journey

Before we delve into the Love Lies themselves, explore where they come from, how they affect us, and the behaviors and ways of engaging with men that they've spawned, I want to prepare you for this journey.

t first glance it might seem that you've heard similar concepts covered in other relationship books, but if you remain open to it, you'll find that this particular combination of dysfunctional relationship beliefs hasn't been presented together before. So you'll want to prepare yourself to possibly be stretched, challenged, and even confronted by perspectives that may seem very counterintuitive, and even radical, in some instances.

Throughout *The Love Lies* you'll be encountering both new terms and familiar terms re-purposed in new ways, both of which are necessary to support your understanding of this new relationships model. You'll encounter terms, also known as "Debrena-isms," such as: *being in your girl* versus *being in your woman*; the *clench reaction*; *scorecarding*; the *insanity cycle*; *energy units*; *seasoning a man*; Love STDs (socially transmitted delusions), and *Manese* and *Womanese*. As you know, the vagina has many nicknames—many not so attractive, and some that are downright repulsive. In this book we upgraded the language that references the vagina and will use the positive nickname "Goodness" instead.

How this Book Is Organized

This book has been written in three main parts. This format is intended to help you effectively understand the Love Lies and their corresponding Love

Truths, and then begin to detox yourself of the Love Lies. In Part 1, Laying the Foundation, Chapters One and Two serve as an orientation that gets you properly equipped for this journey—mentally, emotionally, and spiritually—and ready to open your mind and heart.

In Part 2, The Love Lies Exposed, each of the chapters follows a consistent structure. In Chapters Three through Twelve, you are first introduced to each Love Lie, starting with the Core Four, then to each Lie's accompanying Love Truth, and then to an exercise, tool, or assignment to help you "step out of" the Love Lie and begin to "step into" the Love Truth.

In the final part of the book, Let the Detox Begin!, Chapters Thirteen through Twenty introduce you to the six-part B.L.I.S.S.S. Healing & Awareness Program. This is the section where you get to roll up your sleeves and do the no-nonsense divine self-work that is essential to transforming your beliefs and behaviors, and liberating yourself from the Love Lies. You get to develop and strengthen some new muscles, so to speak. The six parts of the B.L.I.S.S.S. program move you through a detox process to shed the residue of the Love Lies and help you apply, practice, and anchor the Love Truths in your beliefs, thoughts, and behavior.

Preparation for this journey means being willing to unhinge the mask that may be hiding secret pain and frustration, a mask behind which you may be trying to keep up appearances. At the time the Love Lies were being "given" to me, I was in denial. As I mentioned earlier, with all of the personal growth and spiritual development work I'd done, the courses and retreats I'd designed and led, and of course, the two best-selling books I'd written, I thought I was *above* the Love Lies. I thought they applied to *other* females, but not to me. I had to put aside this arrogant attitude, humble myself, and be willing to be more committed to getting free than "being right" or thinking I already had it all figured out. Clearly, I didn't.

As you move through this book, if you find that there are certain concepts or topics that invoke a visceral reaction, "get a rise" out of you, or even stir up some major internal resistance, I actually consider this a *good* thing. Why? Because most likely, what's in a blind spot is being exposed, and/or a hot button or an unexplored aspect of your beliefs or behaviors is being challenged. So if this occurs, instead of breezing over it or rushing through it, *slow down and take notice*. You might even circle, underline, or flag it as a concept that, for you, probably holds even greater learning potential.

How To Get the Most Out of This Book

If you've read my two previous books, *Sacred Pampering Principles* and *All the Joy You Can Stand*, then you know that it is my intent to write books that are interactive. In other words, don't just read this book—engage with it. Keep a pen or pencil and a highlighter handy as you move through its pages: highlight passages, jot down notes in the margins, and underline sentences that strike you. Actually do the exercises and quizzes and put the awareness tools to use.

At the DidYouBuyTheLoveLies.com website, you can access more growth-supporting tools and resources that include reflective journaling exercises, self-assessments, compare/contrast charts, checklists, affirmations, and testimonies from Love Academy participants.

The companion workbook
If you don't want to or can't write in your book, you can download and print a copy of the companion workbook, found at DidYouBuyTheLoveLies. com. The workbook correlates with the exercises in the book. Additionally, I encourage you to go ahead and get yourself a designated journal as well as a three-ring notebook, so that you can print all or select pages of the workbook, hole-punch them, and have them in your notebook as well.

I recommend that you read this book along with a few other people, if possible. You can certainly read it solo, but when you read it with friends you have sounding boards with whom to discuss the concepts, exercises, Love Lies, and Love Truths. You have others with whom to practice the new skills, teachings, and principles. Even better, you may choose to serve as host of a "Vitamin D" gathering—a group of three or more friends that gather for book discussion and dialogue (more on this at the end of the book), and to support one another in the detox process. For this reason, I also include a reading guide with questions on DidYouBuyTheLoveLies.com.

My Appreciation Gift to You: If your Vitamin D gathering or book club has seven or more women, including you, then you can arrange for me to call in to your gathering via speakerphone, a teleconference call, or a video conference link. I am glad to lead a free 15-minute "Questions & Answers" session with your group. You can email my assistant at Info@DidYouBuyTheLoveLies.com to coordinate these arrangements.

Chapter Two

Origins of the Love Lies

I was surprised to uncover the origins of the female Love Lies, the many methods and mediums used to "install" them, and how they are reinforced and perpetuated. The Love Lies are then passed on through female generational lines, through witnessing the choices, behaviors, and ways of relating modeled by other women—our mothers, grandmothers, aunties, older women, caregivers, or other females around us.

They are also "installed" through unsuspecting mediums and methods that include toys (yes, toys!), TV sitcoms, cartoons, women's magazines, religion, movies, romance novels, and song lyrics.

I've developed an "Acculturation Timeline" that enables you to see how and when the female Love Lies are "installed, " and how they are constantly strengthened and reinforced over the course of your first 35 years and beyond. You might be surprised, as I was, to discover that the tender young age of three is the approximate age at which the unconscious, yet systematic love relationships "programming" begins for both little girls and little boys in this country.

The tentacles of the Love Lies have most likely reached out to affect you in some shape or form if you were raised in the United States. Thus it's more likely not a question of *if* you've been "infected" with the Love Lies, but *to what degree.* My research shows that this Acculturation Timeline is more likely to apply to you if you were born in or between the years of 1950 and 1986. Variations in your degree of "infection" may be the generation in which you were born; amount of exposure to mainstream TV shows, movies, and magazines; whether or not you experienced a traditional K-12 classroom education; or if perhaps you were fortunate to have an enlightened mentor or coach who took you through an intentional "detox" process.

Since this is a general timeline, you may notice some variances in your personal experience in comparison to the timeline and the methods by which the Love Lies are installed. For example, we know that TV shows, sitcoms, magazines, and movies you grew up with may change by name from era to era. What's most important to notice is the consistent messaging and themes they communicated.

This timeline's specific focus is on the first 10 foundational Love Lies, though the other 15 female Love Lies are also being installed simultaneously.

The Acculturation Timeline

Age 3–5

A little girl receives her first special toy as a gift, most often purchased by her mother, grandmother, or female relative. This special toy is a baby doll—a replica of a helpless human infant, usually newborn to six months of age. Prompted by her mother or another well-meaning female, she is impelled and encouraged to be a nurturer and caretaker as if this toy were a real human infant instead of a toy. The little girl, who might have been an infant herself less than 60 months ago, starts interacting in full "doing" mode with her baby doll as if she were its mini-Mommy, complete with diaper changes, clothing changes, hair combing, burping, feeding, rocking to sleep, and being laid down for a nap in a toy crib. If the baby doll is found lying on the floor, or hasn't yet had one of her daily feedings, for example, it often invokes an admonishing comment from the little girl's mother: "You want to be a good Mommy so you shouldn't leave your baby lying on the floor," or "You should feed your baby so that she doesn't starve."

Messaging: Though seemingly innocent, an internal "template" is being formed that later influences and shapes her behavior in her relationships with others—she learns that to cater, nurture, and put other's needs before her own is what receives applause, accolades, and "brownie points," especially in the eyes of other females. We can conclude that personal validation and our primary value is based in accommodating and anticipating others' physical and emotional needs. Her young mind quietly deduces that her value comes from taking on a secondary or "supporting role" based in doing for and caretaking of others. This can later become the basis for a warped understanding of love in relationships that tells us that we must sacrifice and forego something of ourselves in order for others around us to be happy. An interpretation of sacrifice as loss so that another can gain starts to set in, as well as what evolves into the I-Am-the-Follower Love Lie later on.

Ages 6–10

The infant baby doll toy is now replaced with a new doll—the Barbie doll or an equivalent. Now in grade school, the little girl migrates from "mothering" and caretaking to a new set of messages and behaviors: now it's all about personal image and appearances. Her new focus is on keeping up with Barbie's outfit changes, Barbie's latest doll house amenities, or asking for a Beach Barbie, Cheerleader Barbie, Pediatrician Barbie, or Ice Skater Barbie, and the list goes on. A Barbie doll exemplifies the "perfect" female body, and the "perfect" face, hair, makeup, and accessories. Barbie is image-obsessed and a Material Girl, and she teaches us to want to be so also. Not to mention that there is also a full line of Barbie play makeup, jewelry, and high-heeled "big girl" shoes. (I can remember so badly wanting the Barbie Beach House and red Corvette I saw on TV commercials on Saturday mornings. I didn't get either of them.)

This particular five-year span is also the period in which she usually watches her first Disney movies—*Cinderella*, *Snow White*, *Sleeping Beauty*, *Rapunzel*, *The Little Mermaid*, or the like. The plots of this genre of Disney films with female protagonists is "scarily similar." These movies present a handsome prince or noble warrior as the female's "ticket to happiness." After first becoming enchanted by her beauty, he either saves her from danger or liberates her from a confined or impoverished life. The female protagonist falls in love with him, and the implication, as they ride off into the sunset together, is that she is now complete and can live "happily ever after." Thus, the little girl becomes heavily invested in her appearance and image as she learns that this is the key to getting his attention, and there is reward in placing inordinate emphasis on her external self.

Messaging: She receives the nonverbal and verbal cues that "looking perfect" on the outside is what matters most. What's on the inside and how you feel about yourself is secondary to having the right image. Self-love is perceived and treated as optional. Love begins to be perceived as something to "get" from another, *if* you have the right look. She can begin to believe, "I am not complete without a male to make me happy, save me, rescue me, or marry me. Someday my prince will come, and *then* I can be happy and fulfilled." The Love-Is-Found, A-Man-Completes-Me, and I-Have-a-Sole-Soul-Mate Love Lies are set in motion; the I-Am-the-Follower Love Lie is reinforced.

Ages 11–15

This is the era of the after-school shows, which typically feature a female star and her slightly aloof, naïve, or "clueless" best friend/sidekick. The setting is usually junior high or high school. The plots of these after-school shows usually involve the girl having a crush from afar on a popular "jock" or "cool guy" at school. He seems to fulfill her fantasy list of requirements (derived from her early Disney movie influence), though she may not have had even so much as a full conversation with him. She is depicted as frequently feeling inferior, insecure, or highly self-conscious about him ever liking her. She puts forth tremendous effort trying to get her crush's attention—dropping her books, playing coy, feigning helplessness, faking a need for his tutoring help though she may be smarter than he is, slipping a note into his locker, and even changing her appearance to get his attention.

Messaging: It is necessary to put forth inordinate amounts of energy and effort to get a guy's attention, including acting helpless, manipulating with feminine wiles, or flat-out chasing or pursuing him. Again, the messaging is that she is incomplete and unhappy without the attention of the "prize" male. The Love-Is-Found Love Lie is further reinforced at this stage, and the notion of the Requirements List starts to form.

Ages 16–21

This is the era of teen or fashion magazines and teen romance movies. We flip through the magazines, not really reading the words, but to view images of our actor, performer, or sports star heartthrobs, to check out the trends in hair, makeup, and fashion, or to see who's coupled up for the moment. There may even be articles on the 10 steps to attracting a boy or how to flirt effectively.

This is also the college-age era. Movies targeting this age group often depict a female protagonist who is average or geeky looking, creative, a great guy pal, and a loyal friend. The popular guy she's friends with, that she truthfully really likes, keeps overlooking her and chasing after the popular cheerleader type who often has a nasty personality and her usual submissive groupies hanging around. She fantasizes about him in the privacy of her mind while maintaining the air of being a girl pal when she's around him. By the end of the show, the guy finally "sees the light" and starts to notice the overlooked loyal girl pal, but only after a devoted female friend gives her a makeover. He does a double-take when he sees her after her makeover. He finally "sees" her for the first time now that he realizes she has the potential to be pretty. It is only then that she gains his attention as a romantic-interest candidate.

Messaging: It's about following his lead and hanging around him until he notices. Form, not substance, is what guys want. Neither intelligence, integrity, nor character matters. Looks matter most. Self-love doesn't matter— it's primarily about capturing his attention with your looks. We can admire the popular guy, or the guy who's the supposed "catch," from afar. He represents an ideal we're holding in our heads; we fantasize about him internally because we feel "less than" and lock on to him as The One in the safety of our minds. We buy the I-Have-a-Sole-Soul-Mate and the Self-love-Is-Optional Love Lies. We begin lengthening our Requirements List, and the "standards" for our Expectations List begin to form.

Ages 22–26

This is the era when she transitions to reading or skimming through celebrity lifestyle and gossip magazines (often in the grocery store check-out aisle). The titles on the front covers of the magazines targeting this age group always mention relationships: the emphasis is on who's dating whom, who's broken up with whom, or who's sexing whom. Even perusing the headlines, the titles focus your attention on being desirable to a man, and "catching" or "getting" a man. The night club life—alcohol, music, dancing, and "hooking up"—is glorified. A young woman can find herself living vicariously through the tumultuous love lives of celebrities, or romance novels with their high drama, perfectly romantic love scenes, and glamorous characters, and yearning for what appears to be a fairytale outcome, which includes a big ring and a lavish wedding. She becomes more self-conscious about whether or not any guys are asking her out on dates. On Valentine's Day, the holiday that capitalizes the most on the I-Have-a-Sole-Soul-Mate Love Lie, she now starts to be highly aware of whether or not she has a "special someone" to share this day with.

Messaging: It's time to be on a serious search for The One, similar to the celebs that seem to go through each other like disposable cups. Time to think about "getting swept off of my feet" and to start thinking seriously about marriage. The way to find The One is to keep dating and discarding men until The One is found. You should now be lengthening your Requirements List, and honing your "expectations" of a man so that you "know" when you "find" him. Dating is the sort, screen, and reject process that gets you closer and closer to The One. He who "scores highest" on your Requirements List must be The One. The Dating-Is-How-I-Really-Get-to-Know-Him Lie is set in motion, and the Requirements List, Expectations List, and I-Have-a-Soul-Mate Love Lies are further reinforced.

Ages 27–35

This is the era when, frequently, a woman becomes engrossed in "more sophisticated" women's magazines such as *Vogue, Glamour, Essence, Cosmopolitan, Ebony,* or *Vanity Fair,* all featuring articles on how to have more romance in her life. She becomes reliant on this formulaic advice in order to "find" her soul mate. In line with her Love Lies programming, she now starts to be concerned about "getting too old" to have a baby or not meeting The One by her 30th birthday (and if she's 35 or older, the desperation and feelings of low self-worth set in).

If she hasn't already, she begins to watch romantic comedies, often referred to as the "chick flick" genre of movies, to satiate this inner longing. The chick flick movie plots play perfectly into the hands of the dysfunctional Love Lies programming and to the yearning and longing they create within women. You're probably well-acquainted with the "scarily similar" story line: girl serendipitously meets guy, locks eyes, and falls in love after a very short period of time (a period that almost always includes sex). It's love at first sight.

Subsequent scenes show a montage of "bonding moments" using a time-lapsed slow-motion technique that shows images of deep-eye-gazing moments and a series of romantic encounters over a condensed period of time. Often, the closing slow-motion scene shows them entering into a sex scene, or it shows the "morning after," where the assumption is that they've had sex. The movie plot depicts the guy saying and doing the perfect thing, having perfect timing, being perfectly romantic and affectionate, and then him finally confessing his love, all within a matter of weeks. Chick flick movies usually end with a confession of true love, a marriage proposal, or a wedding ceremony.

Messaging: A few candlelight dinners, a picnic, a stroll on the beach with rolled up pant legs and bare feet, and a couple of shared interests make for true love and lead to a marriage proposal and longevity. We find ourselves yearning for a guy who magically already knows how to be perfectly in synch with us, like the images so carefully crafted in the love stories and chick flicks. And, of course, we believe that the guy who already knows must be The One. Love is depicted as mutual sexual attraction. No emotional or spiritual maturity is required on the part of either party, just sexual attraction. Sexual attraction is confused with being in love, and we believe that sex can serve as the glue of the relationship. The He-Should-Already-Know and the "supposed to's" of the Expectations Love Lies are now in full swing.

Age 36 and beyond

Based on what we hear, see, and overhear, and when we compare notes with other females, we become convinced that men are fixed and static. "You know how men are" and "you can't change a man" are common statements issued from the lips of females, especially during venting and ranting sessions with female friends. The complaints among females are consistently similar.

Since the stories and experiences of other females corroborate as evidence and the frustrations with men are the common denominator, then I-Can't-Change-a-Man seems to be true.

Add water, stir, and repeat . . . again and again and again. Get the picture?

In my live Love Academy courses I've worked with hundreds of women ranging in age from 25 to 72, and guess what? *The patterns of behavior we exhibit in relationships, the expectations we have of men, and the types of male/female conflicts and challenges we experience are eerily the same and "scarily similar" from female to female.* Though the social norms, generational morals, and the means by which the Love Lies are instilled may vary among age groups, the female Love Lies messaging remains surprisingly intact.

With this said, let's move on to Love Lie #1, The Big Lie.

Part 2

The Love Lies Exposed

Chapter Three

Love Lie #1: Love Is Found

The first four Love Lies constitute the four pillars upon which all the other Love Lies rest. Metaphorically, the four pillar Love Lies make up the equivalent of the trunk of the Love Lies tree, while the other six Love Lies are like its branches.

I've nicknamed Love Lie #1 *the biggest lie* because it makes up the largest portion of the tree trunk, informs the rest of the Love Lies, and reveals our fundamental misunderstanding about and misperception of love.

Love Lie #1 is *Love Is Found*. This lie perfectly illustrates how we apply Western-American concepts of materialism to love and our relationships. Ever notice how we speak of love like something to acquire (i.e., looking for love/trying to find love), like something to be "gotten" from someone else who we think "has" it. However, love is not an acquisition. This perspective taints and infects our entire relationships context in this culture. Our culture is laced with messaging about the incessant search and hunt for love; just listen to the so-called love songs. They should more accurately be named "possession, lust, and ownership" songs, but not love songs.

Eckhart Tolle, in his book *The Power of Now*, echoes the insanity of this warped understanding of love when he explains, "Love is not outside of you; it is deep within you. You can never lose it, and it cannot leave you. It is not dependent on some other body, some external form." I agree with Tolle's observation when he states, "Most people pursue physical pleasure or various forms of psychological gratification because they believe that another outside of themselves can make them happy, or free them from internal feelings of fear or lack." Because we are confused about love, what it is, and how it operates, the Love-Is-Found Love Lie traps us in a futile search.

> *Love is not found. It is experienced within first.*

This Love Lie unknowingly keeps women cycling through differing stages of frustration based in finding/looking for/expecting/wanting love *from* a man, instead of sharing from our overflow *with* a man, what is first experienced within. It keeps us looking for love in all the wrong places, looking for love in so many faces. The biggest lie, the mainstay of our current relationships paradigm, sets us up to continually be disappointed and dissatisfied.

Do you see the big setup of this Love Lie? It has us subconsciously seeking a savior (read: The One) who can bring the answer, the key, or the golden prize of love that will fulfill us—*or so we think*. Though we come up empty-handed and disappointed time after time, we quietly (and not so quietly) hope that the love we "find" in a man can rescue us from a deeply held illusion about our own lack and incompleteness.

Exercise 3.1
Quiz: Busting the Love-Is-Found Lie

Fill in the blank for the following statements, based upon Love Lie #1.
1. The biggest lie, Love Lie #1, metaphorically is like the _trunk_ of a tree.
2. The first four Love Lies are considered the _four pillars / trunk_.
3. What three "isms" of the Western-American culture have warped our understanding of both love and love relationships?
   materialism , _____ , _____
4. The culture perceives love as something to _acquire_ or _be gotten_
5. In the current paradigm, "trying to find" The One often equates to us subconsciously seeking a _savior / golden prize_ .

Love Truth #1
Love Is Experienced Within First, and Then Shared

So here's the truth: We keep seeking what can't be found, and where it can't be found—externally. Love is one of the highest levels of energy that we can experience within, and it operates according to spiritual principles. Spiritual principles are those that apply to what is physically unseen, and non-material, but is real, nonetheless. In a relationship there is a sequence: love is first experienced and found within, and then is shared with, given to, or extended to another. Love is an energy that can be directed to another, "given" to another, shared with another, and received from another. However, it is an illusion that love is taken or gotten from another as if it were a thing. Until love has been experienced within, until you have the first-hand internal experience of the energy of love moving in you and through you, you are not able to extend it to another. You can only share what you have. The Dalai Lama, wise man and high priest of Tibet, echoes this truth in this way: "If you do not have the capacity to love yourself, then there is simply no basis on which to build a sense of caring toward others." Furthermore, if you keep pursuing and trying to find love outside yourself, the experience of deep satisfaction and fulfillment will continue to elude you.

> *Love can be given and received, but not "taken" or "gotten."*

As one of my favorite authors, Osho, East Indian spiritual teacher and author of *Love, Freedom, Aloneness* and many other books, so eloquently shares, "The person who does not love herself will not be able to love anybody else, ever. The first ripple of love has to rise in your (own) heart. If it has not risen for yourself, it cannot rise for anybody else, because everybody else is further away from you." He goes on to explain, "Love is a sharing of overflowing joy. Instead of pursuing and chasing love where it can't be found," Osho urges, "learn the art of removing all that hinders love."

Can you see the futility of our chase and pursuit of love? We continue to yearn, seek, insist, and demand that a man provide to us what is not humanly possible for another human to provide—an internal experience of love within our own being. Until you can come from a place of offering, sharing, and contributing from your overflow and giving from a place of fullness, then you are going to continue to feel an inner restlessness and void, and you won't be able to experience deep satisfaction and fulfillment in your relationships—*ever*.

We must come to understand that love is not a scarce resource, as our cultural materialism would have us think; we must understand that love is an unlimited living force and living energy. As you mature in your spiritual understanding, and as you increasingly experience yourself as lovable, loving, complete, adequate, and acceptable, you recognize that what you draw and attract is consistent with the beliefs, thinking, and level of love energy that is moving through you and emanating from you.

The first love of your life is YOU

In the Love Academy, I pose a question to the participants: How do you behave when you are in love with someone? The answers are usually some version of:

I desire to spend quality time with the other.
I delight in their company.
I listen to them attentively.
I desire to touch them lovingly.
I make time to connect and communicate.
I am forgiving and patient with them.
I say affirming, loving things to them.

Then I turn the question around and ask: How are you behaving in your relationship with yourself? Is this how you are relating to yourself?

Are you spending quality time with yourself?
Are you able to enjoy your own company?
Are you listening to and heeding your inner voice, your intuition?
Are you forgiving and patient with yourself?
Are you touching your own body, tenderly and lovingly?
Are you saying affirming, loving things to yourself, within and out loud?

In our current paradigm, our attention is focused almost exclusively on "the other." Most Love Academy participants have a deeply perplexed look on their faces when I "flip the script" and ask them to examine how they are relating to themselves. Are we exhibiting toward ourselves what we so long for another to exhibit toward us? The Love-Is-Found Love Lie infers that love is obtained externally rather than first cultivated within, through first learning to perceive ourselves as loving, and then relating to ourselves lovingly.

When you are experiencing authentic self-love, you naturally make choices and engage in activities that demonstrate having high regard for yourself. When self-love is *real* within, you are also able to easily and readily recognize the types of behaviors in others or in their interactions with you that are loving and respectful and which are unloving and disrespectful. When self-love is real in your life, you are not able to tolerate disrespect or mental, psychological, or physical abuse. These cannot coexist in the same space. They are too dissimilar.

Until you let the biggest lie die, you will struggle with co-creating and experience a love relationship with another. You may experience a manipulation-ship, a lust relation-ship, or certainly a slowly sinking ship, but not a love relation-ship.

It begins with you

One of my favorite books on recognizing that love is not found externally is *Love 101* by Peter McWilliams. He asserts, "When we are already loving and loved by ourselves . . . we no longer have the burning, aching need to love and be loved—desire, yes, the need, no." When we operate from the Love-Is-Found Love Lie, this is exactly what we see—females with a burning, aching need to love and be loved.

In the opening pages of his book, McWilliams poses this revealing question: "If you were arrested for being kind to yourself, would there be enough evidence to convict you?" Whew! What a great question! Kind treatment is observable and is consistent with self-love.

In the final section of this book, you'll be shown how to begin experiencing authentic self-love within or experiencing it more fully, through a consciousness and a lifestyle based in sacred self-care. But for now, let's look more closely at McWilliams' powerful question and convert it into an exercise where you have the opportunity to do a self-check and determine if there would be enough evidence to convict *you* of being kind and loving to yourself.

Exercise 3.2
Being Kind to Yourself

Reflecting on McWilliams' question, complete this lead-in statement with each of the 10 statements on page 36, and circle Yes or No for each one. Read each statement carefully and be rigorously honest with yourself.

If you were arrested for (insert each of the statements below, one at a time) would there be enough evidence to convict you?

having inner self-talk that is affirming and approving	Yes	No
getting the adequate hours of sleep that you need each night	Yes	No
giving yourself time to get ready in the morning at a relaxed pace	Yes	No
having positive, like-minded, affirming friends	Yes	No
hydrating your body adequately on a daily basis	Yes	No
eating foods that are colorful, nutrient-rich, and life-giving	Yes	No
making self-honoring choices that show that you hold yourself in high regard	Yes	No
consistently making choices that show respect and appreciation for your body	Yes	No
consistently making wise decisions about where you invest your time and energy	Yes	No
lovingly touching your body	Yes	No
beholding your naked body in a full-length mirror comfortably and liking what you see	Yes	No

Take a moment to review how you answered each statement. Remember to not harshly judge yourself, but to notice where you may have answered No. Being kind to yourself is one of the ways to gauge healthy self-love being alive and real in you.

Chapter Four

Love Lie #2: A Man Completes Me

The secret to dismantling the web of Love Lies is like finding that first loose end of yarn in a knitted sweater and continuing to pull on it until the sweater unravels. This Love Lie is one of those loose ends that we want to grab and pull on. As this "sweater" unravels, notice all of the other lies that unravel with it. The Love-Is-Found and A-Man-Completes-Me Love Lies together act as two critical loose ends of yarn.

We've already examined the futility of trying to "find" love outside of ourselves. But why do we buy the biggest lie? The sad truth is that we consider ourselves incomplete until love is found. Love Lie #2 grows out of the illusion that we are partial, deficient, or lacking until we find love in the form of The One who completes us. Once we *find* The One, *finally,* we can be happy.

With Love Lie #1, Love Is Found, we explored our faulty notions about love itself. And now with Love Lie #2, we get to explore our confusion about the nature of relationships, what they're about, and how they work.

The title of Terry McMillan's seminal romance novel and movie, *Waiting to Exhale,* captures the essence of the A-Man-Completes-Me Love Lie—the waiting, deferring, delaying, and "holding pattern" that many of us have in our lives. We are holding our breath and waiting to exhale, and the breath we're holding represents waiting to live full out, waiting to have new life experiences and adventures, and delaying the fuller expression of our gifts and talents, all until The One/Mr. Right comes into our lives. We wait, and wait, and wait to exhale, and hold our breath because we've bought the Love Lie that a man *completes* us instead of *complements* us. In the *Power of Now*, author and spiritual teacher Eckhart Tolle asks, "Are you waiting to start living?" For females who are living out of the A-Man-Completes-Me Love Lie, the answer is a resounding *yes*.

Tolle refers to a kind of anxious waiting. When we believe that we need a man to complete us, instead of living fully *now*, we enter into a defer/delay/wait mentality. This Love Lie will definitely keep us in a restless waiting mode—hoping and searching for the one "out there somewhere" who is the ticket to our happiness. It can keep us focused on the future and creating fantasy scenarios about how we want him to be, how he should act, and what he should look like. I appreciate Tolle's definition of the opposite of this waiting to exhale, *In Joy In Myself* now, not later.

In her book *A Course in Love*, author Joan Gattuso reflects on her delusional "a man completes me" thinking she had as a young woman. "I entered into my earliest intimate relationships as a needy young woman," she confesses, "having fully accepted that I was incomplete without a man. Because of this negative core belief, I failed to see myself as capable of caring for myself, as able to make my own choices, fully express what little sense I had of who I was, or regard myself as complete." She asserts, "When we come from a place of neediness, it is as if we are unconscious, always looking for our own completion in the outer rather than the inner. Therefore, we draw into our lives what is not truly loving and supportive."

How do you know if this Love Lie has gotten its "digs" in you? The words that come out of our mouths are powerful indicators. If you've said it out loud or in written conversation, or if you've ever found yourself thinking . . .

"Once I meet Mr. Right/The One/Am Married, *then* I'll _____"
_____ (fill in the blank),
"As soon as I meet Mr. Right/The One/Am Married, *then* I'll _____
_____" (fill in the blank)

. . . there's a very good chance that Love Lie #2 is at work in your beliefs.

The Love Lie #2 booby trap

A booby trap is a camouflaged trap that you trigger unsuspectingly. Love Lie #2 entangles you in a booby trap that is the by-product of believing that a man completes you. When we seek completion from a man and yearn for completion through a man, we begin to idealize a man, making him larger than life. In this way, Love Lie #2 actually entangles us in a particularly sinister trap—the trap of male idolatry. Yes, that's right! Male idolatry is a dangerous by-product of our prevailing relationships paradigm. If we're not careful, idealizing a man can morph into idolizing a man. The code name for our male idol is Mr. Right/The One or the Soul Mate.

When we idolize a man we put him on a "pedestal of perfection" and we assign fantasy characteristics to him that can be a far cry from the less glamorous but real traits he may have. When we idolize a man, we can dismiss or subvert our own perspectives or values for his; we can become overly dependent upon him emotionally, psychologically, or sexually; or we can violate our own ethics or integrity in an effort to get his attention or please him. We may even allow him to get away with treating us questionably or disrespectfully for fear that we might "lose" him to another female. This Love Lie is a doomed setup that consistently results in an experience of hurt and disappointment. Once his mask cracks or we see his humanness, frailties, and imperfections, we demote him from the pedestal we have him on. This is especially prone to happen when we focus on image, exaggerate his "good" qualities, or feel a need to perceive him as "all that" because it makes us look good or feel better.

When I was in my early 20s, this was my modus operandi: I could feel that there was a void within me. I now realize that my misguided solution was to always to be on the "look-out" for the "perfect catch" (my idol) who would somehow be able to give me an infusion of his love and fill the void within me. I lived in Southern California at the time, and the male idolatry phenomenon was alive and well among females. This made for dates with a lot of guys, and opening my legs too soon and too often to sex, but not a lot of deep and lasting connection.

A Course in Miracles, a profound book of wisdom teachings and spiritual knowledge that's been a staple in my personal library for more than a decade, explains that "behind the search for every idol lies the yearning for completion." In this case, the idol is an external "him" to whom we're looking for completion. A Course in Miracles further explains that "to seek a special person or thing to add to you to make yourself complete, can only mean that you believe some form is missing." The mind trick is that, though it appears so, "it never is the idol that you want, but what you believe the idol offers you." (Italics, mine.) After all, the search outside of yourself for completion implies that you perceive yourself as lacking, deficient, and not whole.

John Baines, in his book *The Science of Love*, elaborates upon this phenomenon further. "Often when a man or woman seeks a partner, he/she is not motivated by love, but by the personal advantages to be gained from love. People may seek love because they want to satisfy the *fantasy* of romantic love and have no idea what is to come after the initial stage of the romantic relationship." (Italics, mine.) Furthermore, Baines explains, they may be suffering from "the weight of loneliness," which can "strongly push a person to participate in a false relationship because she believes the relationship will relieve her loneliness." In fact, she may only be "looking for a way to quiet her feelings of anxiety," he asserts. How many times have we witnessed this to be the case with another woman, or even with ourselves?

I believe that as human beings we are "wired" to innately desire a healthy connection with our own spirit within, with the spirit of other beings, and with the spirit of our Creator. In this country in particular, we attempt to fill and satisfy this yearning with busy-ness, the pursuit of money and material things, and addictions. We can continue trying substitutions in the form of addictions, sex as a "pleasure hit," immersion into excessive technology, and escapism through social media, entertainment, TV, etc.; yet we keep being brought right back to the same unavoidable truth—we're made to desire healthy emotional and spiritual connection with the spirit within, with other beings, and with the Creator's spirit. As long as the idolatry phenomenon continues in our relationships, and as long as we keep seeking fulfillment through things and from a man, we will not be able to experience deep satisfaction and fulfillment.

Who's really doing the completing?

To further illustrate how false this A-Man-Completes-Me Love Lie is, I'm going to walk you through a story that is well-known throughout most of the world. It shows up repeatedly in pop culture. Regardless of your particular faith, whether an atheist or non-Christian, the creation story from the Bible is likely familiar. You've probably heard reference to the creation story countless times.

First, let me point out a few facts that will become increasingly relevant as we continue to dismantle this A-Man-Completes-Me Love Lie.

1. The Creator had a specific order by which Earth and its inhabitants were created. The sequence of creation is intentional, orderly, and relevant.
2. The creation story climaxed with a final culminating creation.

What you probably remember is this sequence of creation: light and darkness was created first; then the sky and the heavens; the earth and the oceans; the vegetation; night and day; the sun, moon, stars, and seasons; the sea creatures, land animals, insects, and reptiles; and then man.

What I've noticed about the Love Lies is that they can cause you to operate on auto-pilot. And when you're operating on auto-pilot, you stop thinking, and a lot can go unnoticed right under your nose. So though you've probably read or heard the creation story numerous times, there are five critical points about it that are especially noteworthy in regard to the A-Man-Completes-Me Love Lie.

1. The order of creation of living things followed increasing levels of complexity, a sequence that moved from simpler to more complex creatures and systems.
2. Eve (not Adam) was the apex and climax of all creation. Creation was incomplete until Eve arrived—woman was the creator's finishing touch and crowning glory.
3. Eve was created in a different manner than Adam. Adam came from soil whereas she was created from living matter, his rib.
4. She was created as Adam's comparable or suitable helpmate/partner. They were equal but different, and were balancing complements to each other. There was no hierarchy or superiority of one over the other. They both, together, were given dominion. They were alike and equal in personhood while different and unique in function.
5. The possibility of human relationship came into being with Eve's creation. She was the fulfillment of the human relationship equation.

We have, in this culture, and especially in the context of religion, used the creation story to justify many untruths. Time and again the messaging we receive, subtly or overtly, is that man is superior, based upon the rationale of Adam being created first. Or that woman is "less than" because she was created second. It has even been used to justify centuries of male dominance and female subjugation. There is a critical detail of the creation story that has often been overlooked and misinterpreted. Let's get it straight—woman is in the completion position! It was Eve, not Adam, who was the latest and final model of human being created. Furthermore, until her arrival, since man was not designed with a womb, as far as we know, there was no way for humans to procreate until Eve arrived on the scene.

Exercise 4.1
Reflections

Reflect on these five often-overlooked aspects of the creation story, and the other insights illuminated here, and share what it means to you and for you.

_____

_____

_____

_____

Love Truth #2
I Am the Completion of Creation and a Living Gift

Woman is the completion of creation. She is complete, by design. But based upon how much we wait to exhale and postpone living full and joyous lives in the name of waiting for The One, obviously most of us didn't get this memo.

I repeat: you are _already_ complete.

Living full out does not have to be deferred. Living full out and embracing life fully should not begin once you are in a love relationship or married, but it should continue.

Now let's take this one step further and put the cherry on top: it's clear from a closer reading of the biblical creation sequence that woman was not only the crowning glory and the apex of creation, but as the completion of creation, she was a _living gift_. She was made special order, so to speak. She was created as a _living gift_ to man, actually presented to man, and made from the living DNA of his side to represent their equality of personhood.

Did you catch this? Woman was presented as a living gift to man.

Imagine, if you will, that wondrous moment when woman, created as the perfect complement and match to man, his perfect anatomical fit, the perfect comparable and suitable partner, was presented to Adam. I imagine Adam beholding this gift standing before him with tears welling up in his eyes, his heart bursting with love, marveling at her curves and shape, her energy and presence, her skin, her radiance. I imagine Adam saying to God, "For me, God?" (Envisioning this wondrous moment was the inspiration for my original poem "The Gift," and a graphically enhanced version can be found at DidYouBuyTheLoveLies.com).

The Gift

God's hand nudged her forward from behind the large, hanging leaf of the palm tree.
There she stood in all of her glory. Radiant.
"Adam, here she is," God said.
And there Adam stood before her
Slowly, adoringly and deliberately taking her in from head to toe
His eyes wide, his mouth agape. Not moving.
There was silence for what seemed like an eternity.
He then fell to his knees, tears now streaming down his face
He leaned forward while on his knees and pressed his forehead
into the ground at her feet,
Sobbing
He then threw back his head with his face to the heavens
With his arms extended with palms up, and out to either side shouting,
"Thank you, Father!"
He was overcome . . . with gratitude . . . with admiration . . . with appreciation
With a deep, soul-stirring love for her.
Here she stood before him,
The crowning glory of all of his Father's creations,
A living gift. For him.
Created for him, created from him, and presented to him, out of love.
God said, Adam, there are special instructions that come with this living gift.
You must remember them always or it will create conflict and unrest between the two of you.
She has been carefully crafted, designed and made with the very best materials I had.
She's been carefully crafted with loving, tender and meticulous attention to every detail.
Her heart has been designed to be able to open wider and wider to you
She contains a special compartment deep within her being called a womb
From which she can incubate and birth new human life
As well as new dreams, visions and ideas.
Her body has been designed as the perfect anatomical complement to yours.
She is designed to receive from you.
She is your comparable and suitable equal but with her own unique sets of gifts.
She has been designed with a complementary set of functions and gifts,
That when they come together with yours inside the covenant relationship of marriage,
They make for the natural ingredients of devine partnership.
She is designed with extra curves—I knew you'd like this
With extra soft skin—I knew you'd really like this
Extra sensitivity
Heightened awareness and A well-developed sixth sense called intuition.
She desires to be adored, loved and cherished by you.
She has a generosity of spirit that is unsurpassed.
She has the ability to encourage you, influence you,
And bring your ideas into manifestation.
When you have her open-hearted love, you will be unstoppable.
She is the feminine representation of Me
As you are the masculine representation of Me.
Joining with her joins Heaven and Earth.
Always remember—she is your equal in personhood
Do not be tempted to subjugate her, treat her as less than, or
Start to convince yourself or her that you are superior. You aren't.
She is a living gift from Me to you.
She is my most advanced and final creation.
She deserves your protection.
She is more precious that the rubies, emeralds and diamonds I buried deep within the Earth.
You are to love her as you love yourself and as you love your own body—
after all, I made her from your own living essence.
Behold her and be reminded of how much I love you.

Enjoy!
Love, God

Take a look at reality shows where a group of women are interacting. Do you see women treating each other like the gifts that they are? Heck no! What you see instead is jealousy, vicious competition, scratching, fist-fights, yelling, hair pulling, arguing, name-calling, back-bitin', bad mouthin', and ugly, immature behavior. This is how female-to-female relationships are modeled and depicted, and what millions are watching in the media circus of reality shows.

It is a sight to behold when you encounter a female who is in her woman, and she gets that she's the gift. She recognizes that she is a gift to man *and* a gift to the planet. And she gets it with humility and takes responsibility for this place of honor. She doesn't misuse it, abuse it, or allow it to devolve into manipulation. She wears it well, she wears it proudly, and she takes it very seriously. It is a powerful "game-changer" to recognize that you are the gift, to recognize that you are already complete, to live full out beginning now, and to stop waiting to exhale.

When you take responsible ownership for being a divine gift, you become a powerful force in your life, family, household, community, town, city, church, workplace, business, and on the planet. Part of being the gift also means that you recognize the power of your radiance, a woman's unique feminine light and glow (more on this a little later).

Exercise 4.2
Recognizing I Am the Gift

Reflections:

How does it make you feel to know that you're a living gift? _powerful._
responsible. accountable.

What are some behaviors you've exhibited in the past because you were unaware of this? _allowing a man to disrespect me b/c I thought I was incomplete._

What are new perspectives, possibilities, and ways of conducting yourself, now that you're aware of this? _I am an extremely valuable gift to a man_

Chapter Five

Love Lie #3: I Have a Sole Soul Mate

*Nearly seven billion human beings live on this
planet with 308 million in the United Sates alone.
Of this 308 million, 152 million are males, and nearly
84 million of these males are between the ages of 20 and
59. Despite these staggering numbers, the I-Have-a-
Sole-Soul-Mate Love Lie, the third of the four Love Lies
pillars, convinces us of something truly crazy.*

We've been bamboozled into believing that there is only one solitary man that has *ever* existed with whom we can *ever* achieve a soul-level connection. This male has the alias of The Soul Mate, Mr. Right, or The One.

If there is a sole soul mate, that means there's only *one* potential mate for each of us, anywhere. So what happens in situations where a tragedy befalls the designated one prematurely in his life, before your paths have crossed? This would mean that the possibility of achieving a soul-level connection is now gone forever for you, since the only one on the planet designated for you has perished. This would then mean that there is no possibility of ever being in a deeply and profoundly connected relationship.

In addition to being preoccupied with finding our soul mate, we're also preoccupied with finding him by a specific age. This certain age is the age by which we ought to be married, or at least have a soul mate prospect on the horizon. What age is this? This age is 30. Not 32, 25, 33, or 38, but 30. I've encountered many females who started freaking out as they neared 30. I hope you'd agree—we're just beginning to know and find out who we really are at age 30. This misconception we've been conditioned to believe causes us to become depressed, resigned, desperate, or fearful: we're told that by this third decade of life our eggs are getting old and fertility will drop off significantly. This feeds the "I should be married by 30" rhetoric. Research doesn't bear this out, however. The vast majority of healthy women who have children in their early and even late 30s have no problems.

Oftentimes, the concern is exacerbated by well-meaning but Love Lies–infected older women or church mothers who say things like, "Why aren't you married yet, honey? Do you have a boyfriend? You're not getting any younger, you know." Or some other form of this statement, implying that "by 30" you should be married or almost married.

The Clench Reaction

The I-Have-a-Sole-Soul-Mate Love Lie can set a very particular dynamic in motion—a certain kind of behavior that I call the Clench Reaction. The Clench Reaction is the needy or desperate quality of energy and behavior a female starts to have and exhibit once she's decided that she really likes a guy, or considers him The One, "marriage material," or a "husband candidate."

I've noticed that the Clench Reaction shows up only at a certain point in the interactions with a guy. This point is when a specific decision has been made internally by the female: I *really* like this guy. She now considers him a serious candidate for a "Relationship." (Yes, that's *relationship* with a capital R). Usually the Clench Reaction shows up after a few dates have occurred, or she has determined that an emotional connection exists, as the result of an exchange of a series of emails, texts, or long phone conversations. She's sized him up and "judged and assessed" his status, education, income, looks, features, and answers to her checklist of questions. He's passed with impressive marks on her internal scorecard.

At this point, the energy flowing from her toward him, and the behavior toward him, usually takes a dramatic turn. She's now deemed him a credible and valid Mr. Right prospect or potential husband material. And since the biggest lie tells us that Love Is Found, and Love Lie #2 has us believing that A Man Completes Me, she begins to think there's ONLY One, so I want to be sure I don't mess this up or miss my one chance.

At this point, the nature of the energy moving from a female toward a male in this scenario takes on to a groping, grasping, or clenching quality. (Think: octopus tentacles.) If this energy were personified it would have hands and fingers that begin to clutch and grab at him. Once we "lock on" to him as the potential Sole Soul Mate, a serious Relationship (with a capital R) prospect, or "husband candidate," we can go from being relaxed, confident, and carefree, to being more self-critical and uptight, wondering if he's seeing anybody else, fantasizing about him, or becoming controlling or possessive for fear that he might lose interest. This is the Clench Reaction kicking in. It's what Eckhart Tolle, author of *The Power of Now*, calls "addictive grasping."

Men can feel and sense this shift, and it is highly repelling to them. If someone were coming at you, groping and grasping, you'd move backward and away. When a man senses this desperate Clench Reaction energy coming at him from a female, he'll usually run in the other direction (and I don't mean this only figuratively). When the Clench energy comes at a man, it puts him on red alert like a screaming police siren.

Unfortunately, once the Clench Reaction kicks in it can lead to us opening our legs to him and giving him entry and access into our body temple too soon or at all. In the recesses of our mind we often think this will increase the chances of him staying, or give him a reason to keep coming back. He'll keep coming back alright, but for sex only.

Love Truth #3
I Have More than One Potential Soul Mate

After reading this Love Truth you now should be rejoicing, relieved, and breathing much easier. Instead of believing in The ONLY One, you recognize that there could possibly be several "ones" out there. For Connie, Love Academy graduate, the most senior graduate of all of the Love Academies to date, this Love Truth changed her life! At the writing of this book, Connie was 74 years old! But she was 72 and widowed when she took the Love Academy 101 Intensive. She'd been married 52 years, since age 17, to her first and only husband, who unfortunately died of cancer three years prior.

I first had the chance to speak with Connie while on break at a women's empowerment seminar I was leading a couple of months prior. At that time she had been a widow for nearly three years. She admitted that she felt depressed and had been walking around for three years with what she called the "poor-me" and "the-poor-little-old-widow" mindset. She'd been around other widowed women her age who advised her, for her own good, to resign herself to being alone the rest of her life. They continued to remind her that at her age there were no quality, available men: they were either already married, were sickly, or wives were outliving their husbands, and thus the number of widowed wives far out-numbered the number of available senior-aged men.

As I shared a few principles with her from the Love Academy during the seminar break, she decided that she wanted to start with some private coaching sessions first, so that she could work through some of her personal blocks and shed this depressing mindset—one that is very common among women her age. She first wanted help breaking out of this funk she'd been in for three years.

In our private client work together I started with her taking her life "off of hold," reconnecting with her passions, re-engaging her joy, and reconnecting with her body, her friends, her interests, and her dreams. Within weeks she had a new pep in her step, a new sparkle in her eye, and her face and skin were glowing. She resumed her direct selling business, started attending women's business networking events, started cultivating new friendships with women who shared her new zest for life, and started walking for exercise two times a week with one of her friends. She even upgraded her wardrobe so that it was more of a reflection of her new attitude, getting rid of clothes that were "frumpy," unflattering, or had her looking like an "old maid."

After we completed her private coaching sessions, she went on to attend the Love Academy 101. It was here she realized that she'd "bought" the I-Have-a-Sole-Soul-Mate Love Lie, lock, stock, and barrel. She'd been believing that her deceased husband was her one and only soul mate, and now that he'd passed away there was no hope or possibility of another deeply connected relationship or marriage. No need to even desire it. It wasn't possible. It wasn't going to happen. It couldn't happen—after all, her sole soul mate had died. At Love Academy she had her blinders blown off. She came to realize that this belief was bogus and that she'd bought a crock of doo-doo. Yes, her husband may have been a soul mate, but that didn't mean that he was her only soul mate. When this Love Lie was exposed, she came to recognize that there could be other soul mate possibilities for her—taking nothing away from the deep connection that she and her husband had shared.

The Love Academy challenged her long-held beliefs and opened her mind. From there she decided to re-open her heart. Both her mind and her heart had been closed. She even explored a couple of online dating accounts that catered to senior citizens. It was through one of these websites that she met her new husband. Within two years of completing Love Academy 101, Connie was a newlywed again, at age 74. She remarried to a man who had lost his spouse

to cancer a few years prior. My husband, Joe, and I were guests at her intimate outdoor wedding ceremony at the Kubota Gardens here in Seattle. It was
inspiring to behold the two of them together—mutual love, giddiness, and
adoration were oozing out of both of them, like they both were in love for the
first time. Connie describes her new relationship as "being made in heaven."
They are living in bliss and she is enjoying life with her new soul mate.

Interestingly, the other most-senior graduate of Love Academy 101,
Karen, is also now a newlywed! I had been a guest on Dr. Karen's radio show
a few months prior, and she was intrigued with the Love Academy principles
I shared on her show. After the show's airing, she told me that she was going
to make a point to attend my next East Coast Love Academy 101. She kept
her word, registered, and drove down from Philadelphia to take the course
in Washington, D.C. At the time, she was 68, and a widow also. Her one and
only husband had passed away two years prior. She too had "bought" the Sole-
Soul-Mate Love Lie, lock, stock, and barrel. Karen came to the Love Academy
believing that she'd be a widow the rest of her life. She left the Love Academy
with new hope, a new gleam in her eye, and with the belief that, yes, it *was*
possible for more than one soul mate to exist. When I spoke with her a year
later she shared how she'd met her new husband four months after completing the course. She also met her husband online. She said that she is so happy
and feels so blessed.

Now, the point of sharing these two stories is not to suggest that you can
take the Love Academy, read this book, open an online dating account, and
within one year, be married. Yes, this *could* happen—don't get me wrong (wink),
even in the face of seemingly overwhelming odds like Connie and Karen were
facing. But the point here is to emphasize that both of these women, both of
whom had the odds stacked against them based upon their ages and their very
limited "pool" of available men, were able to open themselves up to a world of
new possibilities after releasing the I-Have-a-Sole-Soul-Mate Love Lie.

Yes, they both admittedly had a soul-level connection with their former
husbands, but they recognized that it was possible to experience a deep, soul-
level connection again, with another man. Embracing this Love Truth became
the gateway to a new possibility for both of them.

Given the possibilities that exist, we can't be certain how the intersection
with another soul that may be a soul mate is going to look, or how or when
it is going to occur. With both Connie and Karen, at the same time that they
were married to their first husbands, the men who are now their new, second

husbands were living their lives, too. They were coexisting, but in another space and location. Once they released this Love Lie and opened their minds (and hearts) to a new possibility, their circumstances converged consistent with the Love Truth they now embraced.

Exercise 5.1
Recite this Affirmation

I relax, knowing that there is an abundance of men. They are everywhere!
I relax, knowing that a deep soul-level connection is a possibility that is
available to me in the form of more than only one sole, designated man.
I relax knowing there are many possibilities.
I breathe in the knowing that a man complements me,
but doesn't complete me.
I can experience "completeness" within myself,
and am designed to be able to do so.

Chapter Six

Love Lie #4: Self-Love Is Optional

*If I've been conditioned to believe that love is
found outside of myself in another called The One
or The Sole Soul Mate, then that's where my
attention is—on him.*

If I've been conditioned to believe that I am missing something or lacking something, then my attention is on "finding" The One that can complete me, make me whole, and "inject" me with what I've been seeking and perceive myself to be lacking. This extreme focus outside of ourselves causes us to overlook and underestimate the significance of self-love, treating it as optional.

Since our culture promotes the belief that self-love is optional, it's understandable that a majority of love relationship books and magazine articles directed at females focus overwhelmingly on the man. These books and articles often emphasize how to systematically sort through and identify men as "marriage material." They offer tips on how to find a man and keep him interested; how to flirt; and how to look, behave, and talk in order to "catch" Mr. Right or a rich one. They suggest that you can experience deep satisfaction and fulfillment in your relationships, though you struggle with self-love, see yourself as flawed and inadequate, or perceive yourself through a highly self-critical or judgmental lens.

In *Inner Joy*, authors Dr. Harold Bloomfield and Robert Kory describe why self-love can be particularly challenging to us in this culture. I agree. We have a double-edged contradiction where our culture of individualism can have us be overly pre-occupied with an "I-Me-My" self-absorption and distracted by matters deemed important by the ego, while at the same time, females especially, have learned that "self-love is akin to conceit and selfishness." The misguided belief is one of the primary underpinnings of our culture. It's responsible for untold self-forfeiting and self-defeating behaviors, and self-made unhappiness, they explain. The authors even give this condition a name—*anhedonia*. They define anhedonia as "a state of inhibition in which we become resistant to self-discovery, self-love, and experiencing inner joy."

Though it seems like common sense to begin with *you* as the common denominator in all of your relationships, it is clear that starting with self is *un*common. In all of the myriad books on relationships that I've reviewed or read over the years, there are very few that even mention the self-development work I call the divine self-work that is preparation for being in a healthy love relationship with another. Thus this Love Lie convinces us that what's important is to leapfrog over first considering the condition of our primary human relationship, the one with self, and instead, focus on the man as the desired target or object. This is categorically avoided, skipped over, swept under the rug, and treated as insignificant. So why is it that we are so externally directed and preoccupied with the secondary relationship, the one with a man, but not with our primary human relationship with self first? Here are some possibilities:

- You may have to come face to face with a gap between saying that you love yourself and behaviors that reveal otherwise.
- You may uncover a hidden, subterranean stream of self-doubt, anger, guilt, or rage and shame that you've never dealt with.
- You'd rather focus on another instead of take responsibility for addressing and healing your own beliefs, perceptions, and behaviors.
- It requires that you heal from past emotional baggage in the form of pain, resentment, guilt, and shame through active forgiveness work.
- You may be afraid of finding something you consider ugly or horrible if you look too closely. You've come to believe that "the truth hurts" as the justification for focusing outside of yourself. (Actually, it's the lies and delusions that hurt. The truth makes you free!)

In a highly materialistic culture such as ours, we are used to valuing what's physical, tangible, and three-dimensional. However, a love relationship moves us into territory that is foreign to many of us, where we are dealing with the intangible, the unseen, and the nonphysical, also known as the spiritual. Having to address our primary relationship, the one with self, means having to acknowledge that there is preliminary self-work to do, and being willing to do it. This takes time and requires that we first learn to accept, embrace, love, and appreciate ourselves. Not because we're flawed, but because personal cultivation work and spiritual preparation, in the form of healing, forgiveness, and maturing, equips us to experience healthy love in our primary human relationship and then be able to share and experience it in a love relationship with another.

You will notice that this book starts from a different square one. It starts with a focus on YOU instead of on the man.

Are you eligible?

We are familiar with hearing the term "eligible" used in conjunction with a man being an "eligible bachelor," meaning he's single and available. Hearing it used in relation to females is new. So what makes a female eligible to be in a love relationship with a man? As far as I'm concerned, simply being single and available doesn't make you eligible. As I use it here, eligible to be in a love relationship with another means that self-love is first alive and well in your primary love relationship—the one with yourself. As a matter of fact, you can be in a love relationship, or even be married, and still be ineligible!

An eligible female is one whose primary relationship, the one with self, is fortified, loving, and a reflection of the high value she places on her mind, body, energy, time, and spirit. She recognizes that she's *already* in a fulfilling love relationship—the one with herself. She has released insecurities about her body; she has been deliberate about getting healed from her past and/or past relationships; she knows how to sustain being in a state of joy; she is comfortable spending time in her own company; she spends consistent time in stillness and quiet, getting to know herself, learning what feeds her spirit, connecting with her own spirit and the divine spirit of the creator (God, Allah, Jehovah, or the name you give the universal source).

What a seemingly simple notion—to be eligible to be in a love relationship with a man requires that you first know how to be in a healthy relationship with yourself. The truth is that you are ineligible to be in a healthy, fulfilling love relationship with "another self" if the relationship you have with yourself is unhealed and unstable. However, most females are *in*eligible to be in a love relationship with another self (and we keep skipping over this prerequisite) because we have not yet learned how to generate healthy love from within, or how to embrace our bodies without a constantly critical lens of self-judgment and self-condemnation.

As we discussed with Love Lie #1, you must first come to know and experience *internally* that which you want to experience *externally*. Remember, you can give something only when you first *have* it to give and share.

How do you know if self-love is lacking?

Is love present or is criticism present? Are self-acceptance and approval present or self-denigration, criticism, and condemnation? For too many of us, we are not comfortable in our own skin, and we may even have unresolved negative beliefs and emotions associated with being female and born into a female body. This sets a pattern in motion where we can have an unhealthy need or dependence upon external validation, struggle to give or receive love, be fearful of close relationships, default to confusing lust with love, or thinking that more and more sexual experiences can satisfy the desire to experience genuine connection and love. Furthermore, our behaviors can be propelled by an inner deficiency of self-love. This can keep us looking to a man to be the compensation for what we perceive as missing within, or for what we haven't taken responsibility for cultivating within ourselves. This Love Lie then feeds back into the Love-Is-Found and A-Man-Completes-Me Love Lies, creating a sticky web indeed.

This unconscious need to "get" love from a man to compensate for our own internal lack can spawn immature and very unattractive behaviors such as tolerating disrespectful behavior; having clingy or desperate energy or behavior; or becoming emotionally needy and dependent. The Clench Reaction mentioned earlier is also a by-product of a lack of self-love.

When a fundamentally loving and self-honoring relationship with ourselves is missing, we can be plagued by a gnawing inner restlessness, low-grade frustration, a loss of vitality and passion, and inner discontent, despite having material trappings, external beauty, or social achievements. When self-love is not solidly in place, it shows. When self-love is lacking, we are susceptible to being in depleting, stagnant, abusive, or toxic relationships. We can become overly dependent upon others, develop "parasitic" behaviors, manipulate, be overly controlling, or be intensely jealous. When self-love is lacking, we can be insecure or highly judgmental of ourselves and our bodies, even mistreating our bodies with food, alcohol, or drugs. We can suffer from "doing-itis" (remember the timeline, the baby doll, and the mini-Mommy doing-mode that it invokes as early as age three?), a starved spirit, constant busy-ness, a life characterized by a frenetic pace, feeling overwhelmed, trying to people-please, or a constant need to prove ourselves.

When these types of behaviors are present, we certainly aren't eligible to be in a love relationship with another—at least, *not yet.*

Exercise 6.1
Signs of a Lack of Self-love

These are 12 additional characteristics that can manifest when self-love is lacking. For each statement, respond with either "It Applies" or "It Doesn't Apply." For the statement not to apply, it must not apply in its entirety.

- Have a hard time saying no and meaning it
- Feel compelled to justify or rationalize why you said no for fear of disappointing others or letting them down
- Are highly emotionally reactive and/or defensive
- Neglect proper care of your body temple
- Are a people pleaser, to a fault
- Use sex as a power play, or a "carrot" to "keep him coming back"
- Rely heavily on others for validation and approval
- Use your looks, money, or material things to manipulate or control
- Say demeaning things to yourself out loud or in your inner self-talk
- Allow others to disrespect you in word or deed, put you down, or call you names
- Feel unworthy of success or good things happening to you (expecting the other shoe to drop if things get too good)
- Tolerate abuse (physical, sexual, mental, or psychological)

How many of these ring true for you? ___9___. You can be single and be challenged with loving yourself, or you can be married and be challenged with loving yourself. Your relationship *status* doesn't matter. What does matter is that you understand that self-love is not optional, but required.

Love Truth #4
Self-love Is Required

Self-love forms the basis of how you see yourself, perceive others, and how you relate and engage with others. It is not optional, but essential. You may wonder why you keep experiencing certain behaviors from men or why you keep attracting certain types of men. Often the answer can be found by having a truthful exploration of your relationship with yourself. The process of breaking free from the Love Lies begins with you, how you feel about you, how you perceive you, and the health of the relationship you have with you.

Haven't you noticed? In *every* relationship you've ever been in, *you* have always been there!

Divine self-work requires that we become more awake and aware; learn to love and embrace ourselves; and put forth the effort to intentionally and actively heal unhealthy patterns.

How do you know if you truly love yourself? The litmus test is very simple: you are experiencing a state called inner joy as the rule and not the exception. When you are in a state of inner joy, you are experiencing the unimpeded flow of love within you. And the result of this inner flow of love is an accompanying experience of inner peace.

Francesca's story

Francesca, single, age 39, came to a Love Academy 101 Intensive secretly hoping, she later told me, that I would be sharing a list of "man-catching" techniques that she could begin to apply immediately. She walked into the room looking very "matronly," and giving the impression that she was much older than her 39 years. As she was able to admit by the end of the course, she had come in with a self-love crisis, preoccupied (more like obsessed) with finding a man so that she could finally "find" happiness. She even carried her Requirements List around in her purse—one she constantly worked on that had now grown to a whopping 85 items! Very soon into the course, the light bulb came on for her. After the Love-Is-Found, A-Man-Completes-Me, and the Requirements-List Love Lies were revealed and discussed, she came to realize that her

Exercise 6.2
Self-loving Affirmation: Mirror Work

In my journey of self-love, affirmations have played an essential part. Affirmations are positive statements spoken or written in the present tense. They help to upgrade your thinking and re-program your mind when repeated and embraced, as they did for Francesca. Say each affirmation out loud, three times, s-l-o-w-l-y, *while looking into your own eyes in a mirror.*

I love and accept myself. (repeat three times)
I am whole and complete. (repeat three times)

primary relationship, the one she was in with herself, was in disrepair and badly in need of her attention. Francesca realized that "falling in love with herself" was her first order of business, not "finding" a man.

Listen to how Francesca describes her "before and after" transformation, and how making self-love required instead of optional has changed her life.

Before Love Academy, I had very low self-esteem when it came to men. I thought I was too overweight for a man to like me. I was the girl who had to shop in the "chubby" section in stores. Oh, I had friends who were boys, but I was always the "friend" they called for advice about their girlfriends. I didn't date much, but when I did, I would date men who were emotionally unavailable. Or I seemed to pick men who flattered me at first, but became controlling as time went on. I knew these men were not right for me, but I felt it was as good as I was going to get. I felt these were the men who were attracted to me, and I couldn't be choosy. I was overweight, had low self-esteem, and felt that I should be grateful that some man, any man, would give me attention.

At age 39, when I decided to take Love Academy 101, I thought Debrena was going to tell me how to "reel in" a man. Boy, was I wrong. I learned very quickly that Love Academy 101 was, among other things, about loving myself fully first. Through practicing self-care I've started to radiate a feminine power I have never known. I've shed a lot of the limiting, guilt-based hang-ups I inherited from my strict religious upbringing. I take better care of my body. I am starting to incorporate walking at least one to two days a week. I went natural with my hair, wearing no more chemical relaxers. I try to take more baths instead of just showers since they are very relaxing. I get pedicures once a month. I have a confidence about me that shows. I've released weight. I walk taller and with grace and ease.

My eyes have a twinkle in them. I have truly grown my self-love, and it has shown up in my behavior and in my presence. I have filled my mind with affirming things, saying affirmations to myself like, 'I am wonderful. I am sensuous and sexy!'

I now know I am worthy of having a loving man in my life . . . one who will love me for me. I know that loving me and honoring me first is most important.

If you saw Francesca today, you would barely recognize her. She has a sashay to her walk, dresses in bright colors, wears beautiful silk flowers in her hair, lights up the room when she enters, and radiates sensuousness and juiciness. She even competed in a pageant for the first time, the American Beauties Plus Pageant, and won the Queen crown for her category! Now, she comes from a place of sharing and giving love, from her own overflow, instead of looking to fill a void and "get" it from outside herself, from a man.

Exercise 6.3
How Do I Know If I'm Self-loving?

When self-love is absent or scanty within you, there are behaviors that are consistent with a lack of self-love. Likewise, when self-love is real within us, there are behaviors that are consistent with the active presence of self-love. Do the exercise below, to find out where you stand with demonstrated self-love in your life. Read over each statement very carefully, being mindful to assess yourself where you are right now, not where you'd like to be. Check the statements that apply to you.

☑ I approve of myself.

☑ I talk gently and lovingly to myself (out loud or in my inner self-talk).

☑ I trust *and* heed my inner voice, intuition, and inner wisdom. (I listen *and* act on it).

☑ "Being" in a state of inner joy is familiar to me.

☑ I've actively engaged in comprehensive healing and forgiveness processes and exercises to unload emotional baggage from my past.

☑ I have released anger, guilt, shame, resentment, or feelings of rejection from my mind, body, and spirit.

☑ My choices and decisions are aligned with what I claim is important to me.

☑ I like *all* parts of my body.

☑ I am able to experience pleasure from the simple things in life.

☑ I have and continue to develop enriching, supportive, affirming friendships.

☐ I am able to be comfortable accepting thanks, appreciation, appropriate affection, or compliments from others.

☑ I am able to relax and enjoy silence and stillness without getting restless or distracted.

☑ I am able to have fun and laugh heartily without feeling self-conscious.

☑ I am able to rebound from a loss, a defeat, or a disappointment quickly.

Look back over this self-love assessment list of 14 items and count how many statements you were able to check off as affirmative. Write that number here: _13_ .

If you marked six or fewer, consider it a firm nudge to let you know that your relationship with yourself needs some serious attention. Remember, this exercise is about awareness. The goal is to get to the place in your relationship with yourself that you are able to mark off *all* of the items (this is also my aspiration). Right now, you might not be at this place—that's okay. I know that I'm still working on a few of these myself. It's a place to work toward, however, and I'm going to offer some ways for you to do that when we get to Part 3, in the B.L.I.S.S.S. Healing & Awareness Program section of this book, where we'll more deeply explore the power of sacred self-care as a path to self-love.

Chapter Seven

Love Lie #5: My "Requirements List" Ensures that I Find "The One"

Most of us have one . . . I used to.
It's usually in a journal, a purse, or held in your head.
Women's magazines advocate having one.
So do talk-show experts and relationship books.

You *must* have one or you'll never get what you want, we're told, and you certainly will never find Mr. Right. I'm referring to the Requirements List—the checklist of what we have determined are the "requirements" for Mr. Right—you know, things like height, weight, income, eye color, type of hair or hair texture, type of physique, education level, or skin tone.

The Requirements List (heretofore called the List) Love Lie tells us to be clear about what we want in a man. We're told to write it down to make it more real. After all, you have to have a way to recognize him so you can know if he's your soul mate, right? We can find ourselves believing some version of the following: the man who is able to fulfill the most of these "requirements" must be The One, my Sole Soul Mate. The List Love Lie convinces us that it's the list itself that has the power to ensure that we find The One. You are even told how to use your list as a sorting and screening tool to avoid "wasting" time on someone who's clearly *not* The One, right? Without a list to use in shopping for Mr. Right it is not possible to find a good man, much less The One who can complete us. The List serves as the checklist of the "shoulds" that The One is supposed to have. The Lies tell us since there's only one soul mate out there, the List is what you use to identify him and make sure you've found him, and thus found love. The more items checked off, the higher his "score," and thus the more likely he is to be The One. You'll be stuck in an endless loop of looking and searching without your List.

As you read this, you may think, "*This is crazy*. I don't believe this." Yet it is the way of thinking that has infected more of us than not. Though we continue to use the list approach to try to find a good man, it keeps failing us. Has it occurred to us, contrary to popular brainwashing, that having this type of list is at the root of our continuing relationships problem? Has it occurred to us that instead of this type of list getting us closer to deep satisfaction and fulfillment, it seems to be moving us further and further away?

When we're seeking and in "hunt" mode, we're out of order. We, as females, are meant to draw, attract, and magnetize to us. This is why the List, as it stands, continues to give us an experience of disappointment. Worse, these lists are too often based upon fantasy features and ideals derived from romance novels, movies, and especially chick flicks. What the List *does* do is move us closer to harsh judgment, and intensely screening men like they're actors trying out for a movie part, or a potential employee interviewing for a job.

You might be surprised to know that our lists are not original, though we *think* they are. In fact, the same core features and characteristics appear on almost every female's list, again and again, with haunting consistency. For example, the top six "winners" that recur on the lists of Love Academy participants with amazing consistency include some version of:

fine/good-looking/attractive/handsome,
tall,
honest,
a sense of humor,
fun-loving (or likes to try new things),
physically fit, and
financially secure/financially independent.

For Christian women, additional requirements, such as "having a relationship with the Lord, a man who loves the Lord, or a man who attends church regularly," may also appear on the List. It stands to reason that since there is an array of unique females, there would be an array of different requirements on our lists. The evidence tells a different story. If you were to look at a sampling of lists of, let's say, 10 to 20 other females, you'd be amazed to find that the lists are near carbon copies of each other. How could this be? It's because the lists we are writing are arising from the same place—our Love Lies conditioning.

Furthermore, the lists we have mainly consist of features and not qualities. Features are usually fixed aspects of a man and are usually based upon physical characteristics. Height, amount of hair or type of hair, annual income, body build, eye color, and type of job, are all features. If you're going to have a list, a list of desirable *qualities* is much more useful. Qualities usually make up a small portion of our lists, however. Qualities speak to the essential attributes of one's character and being, that then reflect in one's behavior, choices, and self-expression. Since qualities exist internally and then express themselves externally, we glean much more depth, insight, meaning, and relevance by being able to recognize them. Qualities are not fixed and can grow, change, and expand. Examples of qualities include being disciplined, generous, focused, creative, enthusiastic about life, adventurous, energetic, reliable, etc.

If we're not getting what we want in a man or attracting the type of man we want, we tend to add to our requirements lists. We think that a longer list will increase the likelihood of finding The One, right? Remember Francesca, who gets the "Longest List" award when, at Love Academy 101, she proudly unrolled a list with 85 items on it? She was very proud of her list because she had worked on it, constantly refining and changing the items on it. She'd been told by one of the popular women's magazines that her likelihood of finding The One increased if she wrote down her List. I understand—writing something down supports clarity. I'm all for clarity. I invite you to consider, though, that it would serve us better to have clarity about a list that has a *much different focus* and *much different content.*

Why the traditional list tends to fail us

Why do we continue to keep a list even though it is not increasing our success in relationships? It's for three main reasons: because it's one of the staples of our female Love Lies conditioning; there's plenty of agreement for it among females; and it's repeatedly reinforced in women's magazines, and especially in relationship books, TV shows, and movies aimed at single women. What I'd like you to consider here is that a list can be useful, but *not* in this current form and *not* in the current way we use it. The List needs to be repurposed so that it can be a more useful tool that aids us in attracting and sustaining healthy relationships.

The List approach is failing most of us for several additional reasons:

- The Requirements List could serve as your specifications sheet, if you were ordering up a prefabricated man from a Manufacture-A-Fantasy-Man factory like you would a product, but it doesn't tend to work with real human men.
- The List is usually based upon fantasy ideals gleaned from Love Lies programming and the Love STDs, socially transmitted delusions, mentioned earlier.
- The prevailing relationships model asserts that the more criteria he meets, the more likely he is to be The One.
- The List serves as a type of internal scorecard that motivates us to treat men like objects and commodities, scoring and rating them inside of our heads instead of treating them like human beings. The List actually causes us to "commoditize" men.

The List has been an integral part of our current relationships culture, and now it's time to make the critical shift to understanding that *you*, not the list, have the power.

Love Truth #5
I Must Embody What I Want to Attract

We give way too much power to the List, believing that it's the List that is conjuring up a man, and thinking that it is the List itself that has special powers to attract and magnetize men to us. Remember, you are the magnet, not your list. You have the living energy field, not your list. You have the power, not the List. It's you that is affecting other living beings around you, and attracting and drawing to you those with matching energies and vibrations.

Taking this a step further, I've also found that the items on the list and the requirements we have of men tend to be a *compensation for areas that are lacking within ourselves*. Unknowingly, we're looking for a man to have what we don't yet embody. *We're looking for a man to possess qualities that are still "under construction" and are underdeveloped within ourselves.* Circling back to Love Lie #2, this phenomenon reflects how we're looking for a man to complete us, or in this case, to fill our "holes," to compensate for what we don't have, or to compensate for qualities we haven't yet fully cultivated.

Too often our self-perception of where we *think* we are in our own development is out of tune with where we *actually* are. So we can be shocked when we keep attracting what we consider "low-quality" men, or those who exhibit similar patterns of "low-quality" behavior. Consider that these patterns are not accidents or flukes. When you're depleted, enervated, unhealed, lacking self-love, and disconnected within, because of flawed beliefs, past experiences, or low self-esteem, then you emit a low-quality signal or vibration that resonates with and attracts men who also have a matching low-quality vibration.

Contrary to the erroneous belief that having a List is your insurance for finding The One, the truth is that the degree to which you *embody the qualities you "seek"* in a man is the best indicator of your readiness for drawing to you a man who also embodies those qualities. Remember, a quality is a way of being, or an aspect of your personal presence, character, essence, or self-expression. Embodying a quality means that the quality is real in you and observable in your choices, actions, and behaviors. When you embody a quality, the energy of that quality is an integral and inextricable part of your personal presence and energy. Embodying a quality means your magnetism is high for being able to attract and draw to you those who also resonate that same quality.

Become a living magnet for the qualities you want to attract

A new purpose for a new list

If you have a Requirements List or some version of one, I would like you to get it out right now. If you don't have one written down, then I'd like you to write one down. We're going to take the list you have and convert it into a more effective type of list. We're going to re-purpose the list so that it's more useful for you and to you in attracting and magnetizing what you desire.

As I mentioned before, if you're not careful, the List can lead you to focus on a man as if he's an object or commodity that must meet certain specifications. We're going to take your list and convert it into a list that is going to be applied to *you*, not him.

Now I would like to shift your focus, once again, back to you. Instead of spending so much time harshly judging, assessing, and scrutinizing men, we need to take some of this energy and invest it into honest *self*-evaluation.

A List for you

I recommend being clear on what qualities you want to attract in a man, instead of writing, re-writing, and expanding your list in hopes of increasing the chances of getting what you "want." So instead of being disappointed by drawing men to you who keep "falling short" of your Requirements List, or "holding out" for someone who meets your criteria, you can make a powerful move and upgrade yourself. Upgrade your thinking. Upgrade and expand the presence of the desired qualities you want to attract within yourself so that your "attraction signal" for that quality gets stronger.

For example, you may have on your list a "requirement" that says "financially secure." The operative question when making this shift in your thinking is to turn the tables and honestly assess *yourself* against this requirement: Am I financially secure? Am I saving consistently? Do I have at least six months of savings to cover my major expenses?

Oh yeah, often it's much easier to judge someone else rather than hold our own feet to the fire, or to hold ourselves up to the same light that we're holding another to. The notion of *being an embodiment* of our own list's criteria is a radical shift of focus, especially since the Love Lies insist that we focus outwardly, expect to be completed by a man, and use the list to supposedly identify The One.

Once you change your perspective and your lens and have the opportunity to honestly self-evaluate, you may find that you might not be doing as well as you thought embodying particular qualities. If what's on your "qualities" list is not showing up in who you're attracting, then it's powerful feedback to let you know that you have some divine self-work to do that supports you in *more fully* embodying that which you want to attract.

Or you may find that you can't measure up to your own standards—the very standards you've set for a man. The statement "I'm not willing to settle" reveals that you don't understand how attraction works. *You can only attract what is consistent with your overall vibration, mindset, and beliefs.* You'll attract consistent with where you *really* are with embodying a quality—not with where you *want* to be, and not where you *think* you are, or would *like* to be. Attracting is occurring whether you're aware of it or not—the question becomes, *what and who* are you attracting?

You can also find this simple list worksheet on the website, or you can take a piece of paper and draw a line down the middle, so that it's split into two equal halves. Write your list, vertically, down the left side of your paper.

One item per line. You can also use the provided worksheet form in the exercise below.

Exercise 7.1
Creating a New, More Powerful List

Step 1: If you don't have a What-I-Want-in-a-Man List already written down somewhere, then this is an opportunity to write yours down—just as it is, without any modifications just yet. If you have an existing one, rewrite it on the worksheet.

Step 2: Read through it and cross out all of the items that are features. Treat a feature as a currently fixed fact. Features are aspects of physical appearance (such as height), type of profession, income, etc.

Step 3. Replace each feature that you cross out with a quality.

Step 4: Review your qualities list, line by line. On the right side of the paper, under the column titled "Rating," rate yourself on each of these qualities on a scale of 1 to 10, with 10 being high.

Your "List" Worksheet	
Qualities	**Rating**
~~Tall~~ kind	10
~~dark~~ loves himself, or preserves	8
~~handsome~~ protects himself	9
~~smells divine~~ affectionate	10
consistent	7
leader	6
expansive	9
collaborative	8
precise decision-maker	6
man of his word	8
loves love	10
romantic	10
thoughtful	9
wise investor	6
good with money	5

Fall 2023

The more that you embody that quality, the higher your self-rating. To what degree is it embodied? To what degree is this quality present and showing up in your life? Giving yourself a 10 rating means that the quality is clearly present and evident in your language, actions, choices, and behavior. For you to give yourself a 10 for any item in your self-rating, the quality can't be a quality that you're working on. Instead, the quality has to be a part of your being and character already.

Here's the litmus test: For each quality, ask what others in your life would give you as a rating. For example, rating yourself a 10 means that you and a roomful of people that know you well would say that you *unequivocally* embody that particular quality. It's real in you.

So what started out as the list that you were using to judge and assess *him*, now becomes an assessment for you. Instead of shopping for a man based upon a contrived Requirements List, you can determine if you are actually ready and able to attract a man that also embodies particular qualities.

Go back through your list and circle the items with the lowest ratings. These can become the focus areas that you begin to work on first, as you upgrade, develop, and refine yourself. This list can thus become a tool for your own self-development and growth.

Chapter Eight

Love Lie # 6: Having Expectations Gets Me What I Want from a Man

Prior to a relationship becoming "defined," meaning the relationship now has a "title" such as couple, partners, officially dating, boyfriend/girlfriend, or engaged, the Requirements List reigns supreme.

However, after the point of having a title to place on the relationship, the Requirements List gives way to the Expectations List. The specific type of expectations we're talking about here are a female's supposed-to's and shoulds that we project onto men.

While the Requirements List is typically focused on fixed characteristics that we want Mr. Right to have and which in turn signal to us that he is supposedly The One, the Expectations List has a greater focus on behavioral and performance standards. It enumerates the behaviors that we have determined a man should exhibit in order to be "in compliance," and in order to make us happy and "meet our needs." To make matters worse, the behavioral standards on the Expectations List usually go uncommunicated to the male. So not only are we holding men to virtually unattainable ideals, but we don't even communicate the expectations to them. The standards we set for men create a toxic cycle—the female continually feeling disappointed because her expectations aren't being met, then the male continually feeling like he's falling short, the cycle of having expectations, failing expectations, disappointment, and the resulting feelings of inadequacy keeps feeding upon itself, all the while, spiraling downward.

I've also found that these expectations are too often a function of the lack a female is experiencing within herself; they are therefore based on what we're not giving to ourselves and want to "get" from a man. Joan Gattuso, in her book

A Course in Love, punctuates this explanation of a man as a needs-filler. "Relationships," she underscores, "are not about filling your needs. A needy person is like a human bloodsucker, seeking nourishment, fulfillment, and completion not in himself or herself, but in you. It is a draining, damaging, dysfunctional means of interaction." I wholeheartedly agree with this assertion.

A need implies a lack that must be filled. Needs, by definition, are based upon perceived deficiencies. When we speak of "getting our needs met" from within the Love Lies paradigm, we're usually referring to "needs" as something we feel we're missing. Looking to a man as a "needs-filler" is a by-product of the Self-Love–Is–Optional Love Lie and is supported by the A-Man-Completes-Me Love Lie.

Oh yes, you have some needs—for oxygen, food, clothing, and shelter. Yes, you have physical needs, and you don't need a man to have these met. These are needs you can meet for yourself, whether a man is present or absent in your life. So what do we really mean when we say "needs?" We're usually talking about five other kinds of needs:

- Emotional Needs: Too often we expect a man to be our *sole* source of emotional fulfillment. Too often we drop our female friendships once we're in a relationship or demote our female friendships to a place of lesser importance. We don't realize that our emotional fulfillment comes in different forms and from many sources, and is fed by a diversity of relationships; instead, we begin to look to a man to be the sole source of 100 percent of our emotional fulfillment.
- Self-Love Needs: We expect him to be the "hole-filler" of the voids within us that only sacred self-care, spiritual connection, and self-love can fill.
- Sexual Needs: We might be deprived of healthy sensuous stimulation in our lives, or healthy loving touch and affection, and thus we begin to crave physical connection and touch. This can lead to us using sex as a "physical connection *fix*," much like a junkie is always looking for her next drug fix.
- Financial Needs: We expect him to be our "money bag" or our "financial ticket" so our own finances may be jacked up.
- Spiritual Needs: We look to a man to be the substitute for a healthy inner connection with our own spirit and intuition, as well as a substitute for the feeding and filling of one's spirit that comes from being connected to the Divine Spirit/Source/Creator/God.

These Love Lies–based expectations are installed shortly after the Love-Is-Found, A-Man-Completes-Me, and I-Have-a-Sole-Soul-Mate Love Lies. I recall watching numerous talk shows in which relationship experts passionately advised females to "communicate your needs to him." This crazy notion is reinforced when experts warn that "without expectations, you won't get your needs met." Again, if we examine our female "needs," we'll tend to find that they are usually derived from a lack of sacred self-care and self-love. The female expects the male to fulfill her emotional and even spiritual needs and fill her inner voids, something a man is humanly not able to do.

In her book *Women Who Run With the Wolves*, a seminal work on feminine power and self-expression, Dr. Clarissa Pinkola Estes describes what happens when we become "needy" and our relationship becomes fraught with unhealthy dependencies. I would call her a female who has "dried up" and lost her juiciness, and concordantly, Dr. Estes would describe her as "feeling powerless, chronically doubtful, blocked, uncertain, faltering, afraid to try the new, becoming conciliatory, nice too easily, and afraid to speak up or speak against." When a female is devoid of a verdant, lush internal life and a foundation of self-love, she becomes susceptible to becoming "needy," and subsequently heaping responsibility for her own joy on a man.

I'm referring here to *unhealthy* expectations—ones that are needs-based and feel like performance standards to a man. Not the general healthy expectations you may have for *yourself*; for example, of expecting to be treated with respect, dignity, and courtesy. If we are in the workplace domain, then performance standards, such as reaching a certain sales quota or completing a certain report on time, where a boss or supervisor is evaluating you on fulfillment of job responsibilities, make sense. But in the domain of love relationships, they don't work. They set in motion cycles of further judgment. In this context, the word *expectation* means "to consider to be obliged," and the Latin root word *obligare*, in this scenario, means to bind. Thus the effect it has on men—them feeling bound, burdened, and heavily judged. After all, who wants to sign up for having to measure up to "performance standards" imposed upon you by the other in your love relationship? Not men. *They hate it.*

Instead of being rigid, needy, uptight, inflexible, or demanding, as a function of having internal expectations masquerading as performance standards, I am suggesting that we fill our own voids and needs, give up our Love Lies–based expectations, and learn to clearly and directly articulate what we like, want, prefer, or desire.

What if you entered into a new female friendship and then found out that your new friend had a Requirements List against which she was harshly judging and assessing you—in her mind, she was cross-examining your clothes, hair, car, level of education, etc. And *then* you find out that she *also* has an Expectations List, a boatload of behavioral and performance standards in the form of ought-to's, have-to's, supposed-to's and "shoulds" that *she's* established for you. *Plus* (yes, there's more!) she has a list of "needs," based upon deficiencies and voids within herself that she expects *you* to fill *for* her. If you knew a potential female friend was operating in this way you'd consider her crazy and run screaming for the hills. And, yep, this is also what most males consider females—crazy. They are on the receiving end of this crazy Love Lies–riddled thinking and behavior.

What males admit behind closed doors about expectations

Few females know what thoughts are going on in the interior of a male, so here's a chance to have some insight. When you read the following sentiments, it's important that you don't go into "internal argument mode" with what's being shared. This isn't about your opinion nor is it about getting defensive. It's about listening and really "taking in" what males have to say about their experience with females. We often are doing most of the talking and it would do us good to close our mouths, open our ears, and learn how to listen, really listen, to males.

After leading live Men-tality 101 and 201 seminars with men around the country, I've noticed consistent sentiments from men regarding their dealings with females. Certainly, there are men who are an exception to these statements. Here, however, we're not talking about the exceptions, we're looking at the experience of most men when dealing with women.

In one Love Academy Men-tality 101 session, Victor, one of the participants, was clearly frustrated and fed up in his marriage. He confessed, "Debrena, it seems that no matter what I do, it's not good enough. It seems there's some invisible yardstick that she's holding me up to in her head with standards that seem hard as hell to attain. It seems that she's never satisfied. I'm doing all I know how to do and it still doesn't seem to be good enough. I just want some peace." As I looked around the room, every other male participant was nodding his head in agreement.

Males perceive females as hard to please. To use a Debrena-ism, in relationships, men consider us hard to please and "un-satisfiable." Most men want two simple things: to please us, and for us to be pleased with them. Instead, they often feel insufficient, inadequate, and as if they are constantly "falling short." They feel that no matter what they do, and no matter how they do it, in most cases, it's still inadequate, especially when they aren't even aware of the unspoken expectations we're requiring them to meet. And I hope you'd agree that it's a lose-lose proposition if husbands, boyfriends, or men in general, feel inadequate in their interactions with us.

A setup for disappointment

When we are judging a man against the "performance standards" of our expectations, it's a setup for him to fall short. We may not be aware of what is coming through in our words, voice inflection, body language, gestures, and facial expressions—however, men pick up on all of these. The way that men interpret the messaging they're receiving from our nonverbal and verbal communication is, "I'm inadequate. I'm disappointing you. I'm not measuring up. Nothing I do seems to be good enough for you." And the net effect of this messaging over time can be extremely damaging and devastating to a man's spirit, sense of self, manhood, and self-confidence. Men don't complain and vent like women do. They just "take it" and keep it pushin'. All the while, it is taking a toll. It can erode his confidence and he can start to withdraw or become passive, build up anger, or engage in addictive behavior to relieve the stress. Eventually, over time, it can even manifest as health problems.

Exercise 8.1
Reflections on Expectations

Stop and think for a moment. What expectations have you been holding in your head? *That I will be the center of attention at all times, and we will do everything my way.*

Love Truth #6
I Must Create What I Want to Experience

When a female is operating from this Love Truth, instead of touting heavy-handed expectations and wanting a man to fill the voids within her, she recognizes that she has the ability *and* power to affect and impact the experience she wants to have in her relationship. She moves from being "at affect" to being "at cause." She has given some deep thought to what she wants to experience in her relationship, as opposed to being overly focused on a Requirements List or performance standards in the form of expectations.

She understands that there is another way to approach getting what she wants—it is to shift her attention to a broader, dual focus of 1) upgrading her communication skills to being "bilingual," and also 2) learning how to impact the quality of her experience in her relationships by doing what I call "bringing the mangoes." This Love Truth addresses both.

Communicating your desires, wants, likes, and preferences
I want to introduce you to two terms that characterize gender-oriented modes of communicating: "Womanese" and "Manese." One of my girlfriends came up with the nickname "Manese" a few years ago when we were having a conversation about the differences between male and female communication in relationships. In relationships, Womanese is a female's "native tongue" and familiar mode and style of communicating, while Manese is a male's "native tongue."

Womanese is the purpose and style of communication she brings to her relationships that is first nature to a woman, based upon her social conditioning and the influencing conditions of her upbringing. Womanese tends to be characterized by inference, being indirect, descriptive, narrative, experience-centered, process-focused, and relational.

Manese is the purpose and style of communication he brings to a relationship that is first nature to him, based upon his social conditioning and the influencing conditions of his upbringing. Manese tends to be literal, direct, actionable, result-centered, and solution-oriented.

Learning to speak Manese and thus becoming bilingual is a powerful tool that can facilitate you bringing about and making real the quality of experience you desire to have in your relationship.

In the first part of this Love Truth, you're going to learn to speak Manese, and specifically, how to put forth requests to men in Manese. This important skill empowers you to relinquish your grip on feeling that having expectations is how you "get" what you want, and gives you a communications tool that supports you in effectively articulating what you want, like, desire, or prefer, in a way that a man understands his part in the fulfillment of the request, and thus increases the likelihood that you will get it.

Your relationship can experience a quantum leap when you become bilingual and upgrade your communication skills. By evolving your communication skills you elevate how you two are relating and engaging, and greatly diminish the communication frustrations and breakdowns.

An introduction to becoming "bilingual" in your relationship

There are three major distinctions between males and females regarding verbal communication. They use communication (1) for different purposes and reasons, (2) in different ways, and (3) with different styles. If you're not aware of this, and/or you haven't upgraded your communication skills to being bilingual and speaking Manese, then you are probably experiencing unnecessarily high levels of mutual communication frustration and conflict.

Given how critical communication is to the quality of your relationship connection it's paramount that you devote time to upgrading your bilingual skills. As was mentioned earlier, being able to speak Manese equips you to articulate what you want, like, desire, or prefer in a way that a man understands so that he can then respond more effectively. A little later on in this book, you'll have a chance to practice speaking Manese.

Males tend to use words to transmit facts or information rather than transmitting emotions through words. They tend to be literal, actionable, and direct in their communication. These male styles of communication transfer from the workplace and the sports field to their relationships. We often consider them to be raw or crass, even insensitive, when in reality they are saying it in the same way they'd communicate in the workplace or sports domains. It is the speaking style they employ when interacting with other men.

They say what they mean and they mean what they say, and infer very little or not at all. Not only their verbal communication but also their thinking tends to be action-based. Men tend to think in terms of results and solutions, and they tend to process their world through an "action lens." Another way to say this is that men often live in a "verb" world.

In relationships, males can perceive questions raised by a female as a challenge to their decisions, ideas, capability, expertise, or authority. A female can overwhelm a male with a waterfall of questions in the name of seeking clarification and simply trying to understand. However, in his male world, he interprets her questions very differently—as a challenge to him or his idea. Especially in marriage, notice how questions posed by you, and usually raised *right after* he shares an idea or a decision, can be met with frustration on his part. Certain responses reveal his perception that you are challenging him or finding fault with his decision or his idea. "Never mind," "Can't you just be supportive?" or "Can't you just listen for a minute without having to pick everything apart?" all indicate this perception. My suggestion: Wait until later and raise your questions at a time that is separate from when he initially shares or presents his idea or solution.

Females tend to use verbal communication to build and maintain relationships, keep peace, describe, narrate, commentate, or communicate emotion. When we're upset, we tend to seek to release and process the emotions associated with an upsetting or angering situation through verbal expression. We call this venting. This is why we often "talk his ear off" or talk our girlfriend's ear off when we're upset. But something else is occurring as this talking is occurring—the talking is therapeutic for us. We are discharging, releasing, and diffusing the emotional energy, and experiencing a feeling of relief as we "get it all out."

We tend to talk to a male in Womanese, as if we're communicating with another female (infer, drop hints, be indirect). We may not realize that we also expect him to respond as a female friend would in many cases. It's important to know that men respond *very* well when spoken to in Manese, their native tongue, and they also respond *very* well to clear requests. We're going to learn how exactly to do this in Chapters Ten and Eighteen.

Bring the mangoes!

Learning to speak Manese is critical in equipping yourself to manifest the experience you want to have in your relationship. There is a second critical ingredient as well, one I call "bringing the mangoes."

"Bring the mangoes" is a catch phrase that represents two slightly different phenomena. When you bring the mangoes, two powerful dynamics are occurring: First, it's about learning to bring forward more fully from *within* yourself the qualities you wish to more fully experience in the relationship.

Second, it's about clarifying the *essence* of what you want to experience "in the space between" in your relationship—in others words, the better, new, or different dynamics that you want to experience. I'll describe what I mean by "the space between" in a moment.

A forewarning here: This next section might be a little challenging to wrap your brain around at first because we're completely shifting the focus from where it ordinarily is in our relationships, *on him as the object,* to *the space between* you and him.

Two keys to bringing about a new and better quality of experience in your relationship are making requests in Manese and learning to bring the mangoes. They are especially powerful when used together. It's simple, yet profound. Let me give you a scenario to illustrate the power of bringing the mangoes.

Let's say you're invited to a potluck by your friend and host Jeffrey, and you're a huge fan of mangoes. As the day of the potluck nears you start to wonder, "Hmmm, is Jeffrey going to have mangoes there? I hope so, I really love mangoes." Then the day of the potluck arrives and you walk into Jeffrey's home with your macaroni and cheese dish. Nearing the table, your eyes scan for mangoes. No mangoes. As each new guest arrives, you ask yourself, "I wonder if *they* brought the mangoes?" Each time Jeffrey walks out of the kitchen you hope that, maybe this time, he will bring a bowl of mangoes to the table. Much to your chagrin, after he's brought all of the food out there are still no mangoes on the table. Disappointed, you go ahead and select from the items that are present.

The next day someone asks you, "So how was Jeffrey's potluck?" You reply with a dejected sigh, "Well, it was pretty good; only problem was he didn't have any mangoes."

Notice how the absence of the mangoes overshadows your experience of the entire potluck? Notice how you might even be disappointed with Jeffrey? He was bringing forth into the space (the table) all that he had to bring forth from the kitchen at that time.

It even bleeds over to diminish your appreciation for the other tasty and delectable items that were present. Because you were locked on to whether or not mangoes were present, you noticed what was absent, not what was present. You waited, watched, hoped, and even yearned for someone else to bring the mangoes. You also failed to recognize that you could "bring to the space" the very "quality" (as represented by the mangoes) that you wanted to experience. After all, that's the best way to ensure that a *quality* is present. You bring it.

Does this analogy illuminate some familiar behaviors?

Too often we wait and look for someone else to bring a certain quality into a relationships space for us—as if a quality is a tangible thing. No, a quality is expressed as a presence and through behaviors. This is similar to the dynamic that fuels the Requirements List Love Lie. The list fosters a cycle of yearning followed by disappointment, much like scouring the table at the potluck looking only for mangoes regardless of the other items that were present and available.

Scenario remix. Now, again, let's say that you're invited to Jeffrey's potluck. You think to yourself: I love the taste of mangoes so I'm going to bring mangoes to the potluck. You recognize that the best way to ensure that mangoes will be present at the potluck is to bring them. That's right—*bring the mangoes*—the kind you like, perfectly ripened the way you like them. Whoo hoo! Bring the mangoes and notice what happens: mangoes are present and available in the space for you to enjoy and to share with others. If someone else also brings the mangoes, great! More mangoes for everyone!

The next day someone asks you, "So how was the potluck?" Your eyes light up. You break out in a huge smile. "There was an abundant array of all this delicious food, and there were also plenty of mangoes. And I love mangoes! Ohhhh, it was wonderful."

The Love Lies set us up to yearn for, hope for, and even expect someone *else* to always bring the mangoes. You can choose to release expectations that equate to demands and obligations, and joyfully and gladly bring the mangoes. In our love relationships, this means that in order to bring a quality into the space, it has to *be present and real in you first.* You can't bring the mangoes unless you have mangoes to bring. When you more fully bring forth a quality you want to more fully experience in your relationship, the presence of it is increased in the relationship.

Want more affirmation, affection, tenderness, loving touch, generosity, and authentic communication? Then bring forth more affirmation, affection, tenderness, loving touch, generosity, and authentic communication. If I want more passion and sexual expression in the space, I need to bring more passion and sexual expression to the space.

Note: This does *not* mean that he can't also. The point is this: when you more fully bring forth a quality, more of it is present and available in the relationship.

Bring the mangoes, part 2

Now we're going to apply the mangoes metaphor to a concept I call "the space between." Below is an exercise designed to shift your attention to a new place—away from preoccupation with the man as the object of your focus, to the space *between* you and a man. This is a major shift from the Love Lies preoccupation with him as the object and focus of all of our attention. The space between may seem insignificant, but it's not. It's the "alive" space between you and another, across which communication flows, connection and sharing happen, touch occurs, and emotions are experienced and exchanged.

Exercise 8.1
Contemplation: Getting Clear

First, the contemplation question to answer is: What qualities do I want to experience more of in the space between me and the other in my relationship? (No writing, just thinking right now.)

Important: please note that I am *not* asking you "What is it you want him to do?" This would be a question from the old relationships paradigm we're leaving behind.

Remember, when certain qualities are brought to the space, the presence of the quality is now more fully present *in* the space. If you bring forth the quality yourself, over time you will most likely find that he begins to respond to what you're bringing to the space. In the current Love Lies paradigm, the crazy thing females tend to do is withhold from the space the very thing we want more of! We want more affection and loving touch, but we withhold affection and loving touch. Since when does subtracting something from the space make more of it present and available? Since when is *not* bringing something to the space a way to have *more* of it? How crazy is that? But this is what we do!

We want high-quality experiences and ways of engaging that bring us deep satisfaction and fulfillment yet we spend little or no time deeply and specifically contemplating what this requires that we bring forth into the relationship. We *do*, however, spend large amounts of time obsessing over the requirements, qualifications, and expectations we have of him. This long-standing approach isn't working!

Exercise 8.2
What Do I Want to Experience "in the Space"

This exercise serves as part 2 to exercise 8.1. I encourage you to get in touch with the deeper part of yourself, the part of you that may often go unheard or ignored. In the space between, what do you want to have actually experience?

At first you may struggle with this question. It's worded rather oddly because it puts the focus in a different place. What you're creating here are the "building blocks" of bringing positive change to your relationship. When you boil it all down, it really is about the *experience* you want to have.

Now describe: What does my deeper self want to experience "in the space between" in my relationship(s)? (This can apply to current or future relationships.) Another way to word this is: What way of engaging and relating do I desire to experience in my relationship?

You get to come up with at least three entries.

1.   *Affection.*

2.   *Freedom.*

3.   *Committed Craftmanship.*

Old Paradigm: The man is the object and focus of your attention
New Paradigm: The attention and focus is on "the space between"

When I first undertook this exercise, I struggled with it. Though I tried to focus on the space between, my mind kept flipping back to focus on my husband. I could quickly and easily describe what I wanted *him* to do differently, how I wanted *him* to act differently, the behaviors I wanted more of *from him*. But this wasn't the assignment. It took me two weeks (yes, two weeks) to answer the actual question without focusing all of my attention on my husband when I attempted to respond to the question. Really take some time and think about this, and not in terms of he/him, but in terms of the experience you desire. Remember to stay focused on the space between. *Stay focused on the space between!*

Chapter Nine

Love Lie #7: Dating Is How I Really Get to Know Him

Females claim that dating is about really getting to know a guy, but in practice and actuality, a date is really about judging and assessing a man to see if he could be a husband candidate, or The One.

This Love Lie works hand in hand with the List and Expectations Love Lies. We believe The One is out there somewhere, and "dating" is how we screen and sort to find him.

When you look at our typical approach to modern dating, however, and what we recognize as the dynamics of dating and how we engage with a man, it becomes apparent that dating isn't about really getting to know a guy, as we claim it is. Instead dating has a very different motive. Particular "pieces of evidence" support this: the "scorecarding" phenomenon that results from the intense scrutiny, the "judging and assessing" of a man that goes on in our heads; the shallow, superficial questions we often ask; our unspoken but true motive to put the onus on the guy to show us a good time and impress us; the sorting and rejecting that occurs based upon his ability to meet our often highly idealized standards, which teeter on the verge of fantasy; and last, the irrefutable trend toward sex by the third date or sooner, and thus giving in to the lust that undermines an authentic process for building respect, establishing true closeness and connection, and eventually love. These all have become common aspects of our typical dating behavior, and all contradict our claim that dating is about really getting to know a guy.

The damage of scorecarding

Scorecarding is a word I use to describe a phenomenon of the current dating paradigm that circles back to the Requirements List Love Lie. A female's internal scorecarding is based on her checklist of items that, supposedly, indicate that he could be marriage material. Throughout the date we're intensely judging and assessing the superficial, much of it based on his answers to a few limited, "canned" questions (more on this later). We're actually keeping score in our heads! This scorecarding also includes determining whether or not he showed you a good time, a determination often based solely on how much money he spent, or to what degree he impressed you.

Unfortunately, scorecarding keeps us from being fully present and keeps us in our heads. It causes us to overlook some potentially important and essential qualities, judge a man within the narrow confines of Love Lies–based requirements, and reduces a man from being a real, multi-dimensional human being to an object or commodity. Oh my—if men only knew!

Beyond the 10 resumé questions

After polling hundreds of females, reviewing heaps of so-called dating books, and reading articles in women's magazines, I have discovered a surprisingly clear and definite trend in the questions we're asking men and we're told to ask men. You might be surprised to know that the same types of canned, fixed questions are being endlessly recycled.

Nothing is wrong with these questions, but according to what we *claim* dating is to accomplish, they fall short. We're not able to get beyond what psychotherapist Ken Page calls a "hyper-focus on externals." Furthermore, these canned questions are often the "fill in the blank" variety rather than open-ended. Open-ended questions support greater sharing of and insight into ideas, interior, thoughts, passions, and dreams. Though we may think we're asking unique, fresh questions, we're not. We're asking questions that are shallow carbon-copies of the questions females have been programmed to ask of men, and we do it en masse.

The following 10 questions represent those that get the most airtime—what I nicknamed the 10 resumé questions. A guy might as well write his answers in resumé form and slide the paper across the table. In an effort to uncover his economic status, income, standard of living, level of education, or job title, for example, we tend to ask one-dimensional, superficial questions right out of the gate. We're not asking questions of substance, which, by their nature, indicate authentic curiosity about deeper aspects and elements of his character, life, thinking, essence, spirit, and what's shaped who he is. We may not even know something as basic and trivial as his middle name, yet after just a few dates (my research shows by the third date, on average) the majority of us are opening our legs, having sex, and allowing a man to enter our bodies!

Here are examples of the canned questions (not in any particular order):

What do you do? (for a career/profession)
How old are you?
Where do you work?
Where do you live?
How long have you worked there?
Where did you go to school? (usually meaning college, not high school)
Do you have any kids?
Have you been married before?
What do you like to do in your spare time/for fun?
What are your five-year goals?

I've tested these 10 resumé question with hundreds of females in Love Academies across the country and taken polls to see how many females have been asking these similar kinds of questions. Naturally, we wish to deny that we are engaging in a series of questions that are obviously formulaic, shallow, and predictable, but my research shows otherwise. So I then pose this question to roomfuls of females in Love Academies across the country. I ask: Ladies, once you ask these 10 resumé questions, share with me, right now, what other questions you are asking to gain more depth and insight into the character, integrity, mindset, and disposition, or attitude of a man? I then ask them to reflect on their conversations with men and to rattle off these questions, popcorn style.

As I scan the room, ready for hands to shoot up with examples of the additional questions pouring forth, there is stillness and heavy silence. They are at a loss. No hands go up. After several moments of pregnant silence and uncomfortable glances around the room, someone usually pipes up and blurts out a question—one that is clearly off the cuff and made up on the spot. Then a few others add their two cents, also making up something in the moment. The question is met with silence because, by and large, we are *not* asking questions out of authentic curiosity. Instead we regurgitate the resumé questions. That's the reason for the pregnant pause. Every time.

We think "*other* women may be asking those shallow questions, but certainly not me," because we want to believe that we are more original, more real, deeper, and more mature than other females. Hate to burst your bubble. We need to stop kidding ourselves. Our intentions and behaviors around dating aren't as aligned with really getting to know him as we'd like to think. And this contributes to an epidemic of women giving up their Goodness too soon and with too little consciousness of the dynamic they're supporting in doing so.

Lust relationships

One could argue that times have changed and social and cultural morals have slackened, and that because of this, females are having sex more readily, frequently, and earlier in a relationship without feeling guilty or "bad." I'm all for being a self-expressed woman (notice I said woman, not girl), but it does not have to mean opening our legs too often or too soon to sex. Interestingly, in a study of 25,000 people published in a recent issue of the *Archives of Sexual Behavior*, researchers found one of the major regrets of women was moving to sex too fast, even in this modern era of so-called sexual liberation.

We live in an instant-gratification culture where sex, very unfortunately, has become "casualized." In my experience and in my opinion, there's no such thing as casual sex, as much as we try to convince ourselves to the contrary in this country. Casual sex is an oxymoron born of the American practice of reducing sex to a commodity and entitlement.

If we left it up to guys, there'd be no dates, no outings, no outlays of money, no courtship—they'd go straight to the "Goodness." Sex is a different experience for them because their sex organs are external. Our sex organs are internal. Think of your vagina, your Goodness, as a gateway. During sex, the male penetrates and we, as females, are penetrated. Our womb acts as a receptacle. When the male ejaculates he deposits a living substance into our body cavity, the womb, that carries energy and an energetic imprint (more on this later). Even if he uses a condom, since he actually entered our body cavity, his energy imprint remains in us.

All too often, when healthy male energy, connection, and interaction is absent in our lives, or platonic loving touch from males is missing in our lives (this includes from fathers, brothers, husbands, or male relatives), we can become "thirsty" for male contact. Many females are missing this healthy male interaction, and having sex is the means for experiencing male touch, having skin contact, and experiencing what, in the moment, feels like true intimacy. We may open our legs and have sex because we've convince ourselves that this means that he really likes us; because we yearn and pine, literally, for physical contact, the exchange of energy, and a deeper connection. We think granting him admittance to our bodies will increase the likelihood of him sticking around. He'll stick around alright—for sex only.

It's incredibly common for us to mistake lust for love. Lust is the energy of strong sexual desire and a strong mutual sexual attraction. One of the simplest ways to distinguish lust from love is to take sex out of the equation of the relationship for a month. Does the communication between the two of you change at all? Does the "climate" of the relationship change at all? Does he start to be less engaged or seem to lose interest? This can be a great litmus test.

The problem is that once sex enters the picture, and especially when it enters too soon, it can easily truncate the quality and depth of the communication that is occurring. The natural flow of open-ended questions you may have been posing prior to sex that were giving you insight into a guy, or even those he may have been asking you, tend to cease. Because sexual attraction is naturally strong and intense, sex can become a dominating factor in a relationship, and can even become the only glue that holds the relationship together. Whatever interest there was in getting to know him and more about deeper aspects of him usually gets eclipsed and even overtaken by the direct and intimate body-to-body energy and nature of sexual intercourse.

In *The Science of Love,* author John Baines explains, "Relationships based solely on sex cannot lead people to happiness or true inner satisfaction." In *Human Nature,* Dr. Victor Brown further explains the by-products of lust. He writes, "Lust prevents and destroys intimacy." Dr. Brown asserts that "lust seeks immediate gratification no matter what the other person feels or no matter what other obligations are violated. It is emotionally incongruent . . . and its consequences are detrimental to self-esteem because lust eroticizes fragments of people . . . always hungering, never satisfied." So what we have in our modern dating approach is an intense level of physical engagement in the form of sexual intercourse taking place with only a shallow level of knowing in place. This "sex-too-soon-sex-too-fast" phenomenon interferes with and can actually undermine the development of true, emotional and spiritual intimacy and closeness.

The effects of the "love hormone"

The hormone oxytocin, also called the human bonding hormone, "love hormone," or "cuddle chemical," is secreted by both males and females during sex but it is released in higher levels by females during sexual arousal and immediately after orgasm. Could it be that this hormone is adding fuel to the fire of the lust-driven behavior that dominates our current dating paradigm? Could we be opening ourselves to sex too fast to get the "love hormone effect"—the feelings of contentment, calmness, security, and the reduction in anxiety it can create? Could it be that we're actually craving the feeling that oxytocin evokes? Have we become "oxytocin junkies" as a substitute for sacred self-care, spiritual connection, and self-love, the same way we buy the Love Lie that A-Man-Completes-Me and then look to a man to fill the love void within us?

When authentic self-love is absent, we may unconsciously look for substitutes. Our craving for this "oxytocin-induced state" or an intense thirst for physical closeness can trap us in a vicious cycle in which we become preoccupied with sex; we may find ourselves acting on sexual attraction and becoming sexually intimate too soon. In many instances we may be starving for both the physical closeness that comes with sex and the feelings of contentment and calm that oxytocin produces.

If we're not careful, we can also use sex as a "false intimacy crutch." *Inner Joy* authors Bloomfield and Kory claim that the "less able we are to experience inner pleasure, the more material symbols we need to satisfy our thirst for it." We need more cars, more addictions, bigger houses, more spectacular movies, and more sex, "because we are shut off—numb to inner joy and the pleasure of everyday living."

The mysteries of your womb

Let's take this conversation about the guise of dating and the rush to sex a step further and consider the physical and spiritual impact upon our bodies, and more specifically, upon our wombs. I consider the uterus, or the woman's womb, the literal center of her body and also the center of her feminine being, her innermost sacred space—the space from which she incubates and grows a new human life, and/or also births her dreams, passions, visions, and creativity. The womb is the inner hollow or body cavity unique to a woman's physiology—representative of the holy of holies, the most sacred space in ancient temples, and also the inner sanctum, the most sacred space within your body temple.

In *The Science of Love*, John Baines explains that "a woman's womb is magnetic, and it actually 'holds' the collective vibrations of men with whom she's had intercourse in the recent or distant past." Vibrations of what, you may ask? Emotional and spiritual vibrations of the men who have penetrated your most holy of holies. Hmm, how often are we the slightest bit concerned with the level of spiritual or emotional energy or even the quality of thoughts of the men with whom we have sex? Are we aware that residual energy from the man or men that have penetrated our wombs can actually accumulate in our wombs? Since when is allowing a man to actually *enter* your body with his body, and thus *become conjoined* to you, a casual act? And it certainly isn't casual when the result can potentially be creating another living, breathing human being. So can we agree that there's no such thing as "casual sex?"

You probably aren't aware how highly receptive your womb is. It is a space within your body that is like a receptacle or bowl (whether or not you've had a hysterectomy) that receives and holds vibrations. When you are entered during the act of sex, you are the receiver. Depending upon which men have entered and penetrated our wombs, and what they've left there in terms of an energetic imprint, our wombs can become repositories for someone else's anger, rage, resentment, self-defeating thoughts, or guilt, as well as our own.

Woman, as the apex of creation, has a womb whereas a man does not. This alone is reason to pay closer attention to this uniquely feminine organ and space within your body. In our traditionally allopathic approach to medicine in the West, we've treated the uterus as just another body part and nothing more. The numbers of hysterectomies in the United States alone are staggering—600,000 hysterectomies are performed each year in the United States. This is both shocking and scary. (If you are interested in exploring womb healing further, I provide some womb-healing references and resources at DidYouBuyTheLoveLies.com to help you begin to reverse the negative impact of the "pollutants" that your womb may be holding.)

Dr. Christiane Northrup, physician and famed women's mind-body wellness author and visionary, in her book *Women's Bodies, Women's Wisdom*, shares her observations and first-hand experiences in treating women in her health care practice. She explains, "Whenever I see a woman with a uterine problem such as fibroid tumors—which are present in 40 percent of

American women—I have her meditate upon wounds that may be stored in her body with regard to relationships, creativity, and her sense of security. She goes on to explain, "Challenges with internal pelvic organs (ovaries, fallopian tubes, uterus) can be related back to a woman feeling stifled, handicapped, or thwarted over time in her ability to create financial and emotional abundance and stability, and to express her creativity fully. The pelvic area is both literally and figuratively creative space. Pelvic disorders are manifestations of blocked energy."

Love Truth #7
Courtship Is How I Really Get to Know Him

Dating is very distinct from my version of modern courtship. The motives and pace are different, and the sexual energy is wisely managed instead of taking over the interaction. This Love Truth shifts us out of the dating paradigm, as we've known it, and into an updated and upgraded version of courtship that meets the needs of our modern era and serves both males and females very well.

If dating can be equated to moving at a speed of 95 miles per hour, courtship would move at 35 to 40 miles an hour. It is time to resurrect and modernize courtship and adapt it to serve and address the realities and challenges of this modern era, maintaining the best of timeless courtship principles, and modifying and updating them to address the dynamics of our over-busy, fast-paced, virtual culture in which one might spend more time looking at a screen on a daily basis than in face-to-face interaction with a live person.

By the way, the principles and benefits of courtship need not be reserved for single women. I am a *major* advocate of date nights for married couples. If you're married and don't already have standing date nights, decide, jointly, when you will begin them, or resume them if it's been a while. For it to qualify as a date night you must *leave the house*—get "beautified" for each other as you did when you were dating before you were married. Notice this distinction—courtship should continue at a higher and different level once you're married, instead of ceasing once you're married. Let's cover the basic courtship principles so that you are clear about how modern courtship differs from our modern approach to dating.

The basic courtship principles

Courtship establishes an incremental pathway and offers a gentle, slower-moving approach to engaging male/female interaction. In courtship, the female's foot is on the accelerator setting the speed, instead of the man's libido or mutual sexual attraction. We are quick to claim that dating is how we get to know a guy, but we've established that this is not what's really happening. It's rhetoric. Modern dating is too often a judge-and-assess, screen-and-sort process that parks at being a lust relationship. Courtship, however, achieves "getting to know" a guy, for real, and supports more relaxed enjoyment; less pressure; less game playin'; deeper, richer communication; less emphasis on sex; and more emphasis on authenticity and truly getting to know each other.

My version of modern courtship fulfills five primary objectives, but first and foremost, hinges upon our ability, as the female, to learn to lead the courtship process and intentionally set the pace and tone of interaction. You'll notice that these objectives are very different from, and in some instances the opposite of, the focus in modern dating.

In the following pages, we are going to go into more depth on each of these aspects of modern courtship so that you can actually increase your understanding, and learn:

1. how to be a great date
2. how to be a great question-asker and listener
3. how to incrementally and gradually progress your outings/interactions/dates
4. how to wisely manage the sexual energy, and
5. how to keep the "energy units" balanced

Being a great date. One major and fundamental shift that I teach regarding basic courtship is about re-purposing the date. When you're operating from the modern courtship principles, then you understand that going on a date is no longer about "being shown a good time" by the guy, and also critically judging and assessing him throughout the entire date. That's old news. Instead, I teach that the purpose of a date, within this modern context of courtship, is primarily about four things. First and foremost, it is an opportunity to learn how be a great date (versus a good date); learn to be fascinated; learn to be present; learn how to listen well; and how to be in your feminine radiance (turning on and keeping on your unique feminine glow).

When you're a good date, the two of you may have had a nice time, enjoyed the activity or event, and had pleasant conversation. When you're a great date, your company was thoroughly enjoyed by a man. He was moved, and even inspired by your energy and radiance, and by being in your presence. When you're a great date, he desires to be in your presence and company again, and very soon.

Your feminine radiance, your uniquely feminine inner light, extends beyond the surface of your skin and gives you a visible, external glow. Others take notice when your light is on. Especially men. The same way that whole, nutrient-rich foods are nourishment to our physical bodies, a woman's radiance is nourishment to a man's spirit. When a male encounters a radiant woman, he responds immediately. He takes notice of this uniquely feminine quality.

There are two very clear and direct ways that you know you're a great date: One is that he tells you. Straight up. He uses the word *great* in his sentence, not the words *good time* or *nice time*. More specifically, he may say, without mincing his words, "I had a great time," but even more powerful is when he says, "Wow, you are great," or "You were a great date." And second, since a man figures that he's not the only man to recognize your greatness, he's looking to ascertain, *while you're still there in his presence*, when your next availability is, and when you two might connect in person again. No need for the promise of a phone call soon or the next day. He's not looking to wait that long. He will be looking to "sew up some new plans with you," *before* you two part company from your first outing.

If he says he's going to call you soon (he's non-specific) and doesn't, or he says when he'll be calling you again and he doesn't, he may very well think you were a good date, but not a great date.

Exercise 9.1
Part 1: Are You a Great Date?

This exercise has two parts. The first part poses questions that help you start to recognize some basic considerations that play a part in being a great date, and the second part gives you a self-assessment so that you can clearly see if you're "there" yet or not, and where there's room for strengthening your great-date "muscles."

These apply when on an in-person, face-to-face "date." Answer YES or NO to each of the following four questions.

1. Are you asking him questions from a place of true curiosity, or from a place of judging and assessing his every answer?
2. How are you listening? (eyes roaming, leaning back or away, distracted, or even worse, having your cell phone ringer *on*, or looking down at your cell phone screen?)
3. Do you know how to "lean in" with your energy and attention, as well as with your body?
4. Does your body language, voice inflection, gestures, and facial expressions make it clear that you're fascinated by what he's sharing? (Remember, learning to be fascinated is not based upon whether or not you like him. It's a form of being present to another person.)

Exercise 9.1
Part 2: How "Strong" Are Your Great-Date Muscles?

This exercise will help you zero in on the elements of being a great date and where you might have room for growth.

Put a checkmark next to the items that are true for you right now.

☑ Your radiance is *on* (you glow).
☑ You take your time getting ready and prepared before your date, and it shows.
☑ You feel comfortable in your body, and you feel good in your body.
☐ You ask questions beyond the 10 resumé questions.
☐ You listen well and are not "in your head" when he's talking or answering.
☑ You smile easily and laugh readily.
☑ You are able to be fascinated and authentically curious.
☐ You know how to be present and attentive instead of distracted and unfocused.
☐ You're able to hear his answers without judgment.
☐ You're able to have a conversation without scorecarding him internally based upon your husband-candidate or marriage-material filter or checklist.
☑ During or after the date, a guy uses the word "great" to describe his time with you.
☑ Before your current date is over, a guy seeks to make plans to reconnect with you.

Out of these 12 characteristics of being a great date, how many checkmarks did you have? Write that number here: _____.

If any went unmarked, what can these tell you about where you might need to strengthen your great-date muscles? _____

_____

_____

As you continue along in this journey, I recommend that you return to this assessment periodically (every six months is good) to see if you're able to checkmark more of these statements. The objective is to be able to check every item as a yes, if this isn't already the case for you.

Being a great question-asker and listener. Courtship holds up to its claim that it is about getting to know a guy. This is why the questions you ask and why you ask them are different within the courtship paradigm compared to the traditional dating paradigm. With courtship, you get to expand your repertoire to include questions that are insightful, thoughtful, arise from a place of sincerity and true curiosity, and are intended to reveal the more meaningful aspects of a man's character, essence, personality, and life, instead of only barraging him with the classic list of canned "biographical" questions that only provide facts about him.

The following questions are provided simply to get your creative juices flowing around questions that are "outside the box" of the shallow resumé questions. By no means do you need to bombard him with all of these questions in one sitting or one encounter, but over time.

For example:

- If you could travel anywhere in the world, where would it be, and why?
- What is one of your fondest memories from your childhood?
- If you could have lunch with any historical figure, who would it be? Why would you choose this particular person?
- If you could send a time capsule into space, what three things would you choose to put in it that best represent you?
- What's your favorite movie, and why?
- If you were given $3 million, tax free, how would you use it?

Remember, these are simply to get your creative juices flowing and to help you recognize that there are tons of questions you can ask that are more aligned with really getting to know him and his essence. Simple but revealing questions like these give you more insight into his character, his thought process, and what's shaped him, his values, and his life outlook, for example.

Another simple way to gain insight into deeper aspects of a man is to ask him to tell you more about something he brings up in conversation. For example, he might mention that he is working on a big project at work, or a new project in his business. First, you have to really be actually listening to catch this, and then you can put forth a statement that will have him share more, such as "Tell me more about the big project at work" or "Tell me more about the new project in your business."

Incrementally and gradually progressing your dates. Energy units is a Debrenaism and a term I created to more effectively explain to females a dimension of relationships we don't or rarely talk about. Energy is an intangible but very real aspect of relationships. However as a materially based culture, we tend to be more ignorant of, uncomfortable or unfamiliar with discussions about nontangible, nonphysical aspects of life. Energy units can take many forms—they can represent time, money, physical touch, sex, and radiance. Yes, even a woman's feminine radiance, her inner light and glow, has energy unit value.

Dating, as we know it and tend to do it, has no regard for or consideration of energy units. The energy units get out of whack out of the gate, starting on the first date, and the imbalance of energy units only gets more pronounced on each successive date. To invoke courtship, however, you start at a gentle, unrushed first level of engagement that requires minimal energy units. And get this, modern courtship is a process that is invoked by the pace and tone set forth by the female. Remember, courtship provides multiple and progressive engagement. How you begin is critical. The pace and tone *you* set initially, as the female, will tend to prevail. In courtship, you lead the process. Start slow. Relax. Take your time. There's no need to rush.

The first level of courtship is the Day Date. A first Day Date need be no more than one hour. Some may argue that you need more than 60 minutes of time energy units to get a sense of someone. No you don't. Test it out for yourself. After your initial 60-minute Day Date in the courtship process, you both will be well aware of whether you want to proceed to another live, in-person date together or not. Likewise, start with a minimal number of money energy units like coffee, tea, or smoothies (should be no more than about $7 to $8 for you, thus seven or eight money energy units) rather than dinner. In modern dating, it is customary for the first date to be dinner, which requires an outlay of considerably more money energy units initially. Hence the energy units go immediately into a significant imbalance.

Courtship moves along in increments, where the next date involves slightly more time energy units and slightly more money energy units. At each level, the time and money energy units can increase, but the point is for them to gradually and slowly increase.

Managing the sexual energy in courtship. Speaking of energy units, another important objective of courtship is that it enables you to more wisely manage the sexual attraction, if it's present, and thus the energy units. Courtship supports you in managing the sexual energy so that you aren't having to suppress, deny, or fight it. In modern dating, this energy is usually running rampant, starting with the dropping of sexual innuendos very early on via texting, emails, or phone calls. Courtship isn't about denying mutual attraction. It's a matter of wisely managing and directing it so it doesn't take over the relationship when it is present. Sexual energy, when it is managed wisely, keeps the electricity and interest alive. The intention is for you to allow it to move you along like a wave in the ocean would carry a boat along, instead of the being overtaken by the wave and then nearly drowning in it.

A date within the process and context of courtship is much more enjoyable and humanizing, and there is much less game-playing, all of which support females in attracting quality males and eventually creating a lasting, juicy love. Courtship also supports both of you in being more relaxed, at ease, and present, and diffuses the tension or attention around the sexual attraction that may exist.

If possible, at least the first two dates should be during daylight hours. In my energy units value system, evening energy units carry more weight than daytime energy units, because we tend to dress differently, spend less money, and generally progress more slowly with physical touch during the daytime as compared to evening. We behave differently in the daytime.

We also behave differently when we're in the presence of other people, which tends to be the case on a daytime date, versus being more isolated and one-on-one, as tends to be the case on an evening date. Therefore, to wisely manage the sexual energy, it's essential that you select outings that put the two of you around other people and in public places. Examples include an outing to a park, festival, fair, a lively restaurant during the day, coffee shop, adult game arcade, or going out with a group of people. Being around other people tends to naturally curb bolder or more aggressive physical touching so that, again, the sexual attraction doesn't start to increase too quickly or "take over" the interaction.

Last but not least, stay *out* of and away from each other's homes. When there is sexual energy present, it is easiest to succumb to it when you're inside one's personal living space, yours or his. Either way, when you're in your home or his, you're in the space where you are most comfortable, the most relaxed, and the most at home. The likelihood of sex occurring once you've entered into a personal living space skyrockets. How many times have we heard the statement "one thing led to another." This is the intensity of sexual attraction at work. This recommendation also applies to meeting up first at your home or his before going out; instead, rendezvous at a neutral place away from either of your homes. If it's between your willpower and the power of sexual attraction, your willpower is most likely going to lose out. Even the willpower of both of you can lose out to the power of sexual attraction. So don't underestimate it, or be naïve.

Do we have plans? You may be wondering why I would include a section on ascertaining whether or not plans with a guy are firm. It's because I've heard enough females lament about this, share their frustrations or pose questions in Dear Abby–type columns to know that we have experienced a lot of exasperation around this. In the current dating paradigm, this is a sore spot. A very different understanding exists between males and females about having plans or not because we operate under differing criteria for whether an outing, plan, or date has been firmly established. Confusion and frustration are common among females because we don't really understand what men consider to be a date or firm plans. In fact, this is one of the glaring areas that reveals our misunderstanding of men. As you leave the dating paradigm behind and step into the modern courtship paradigm, it serves you to be clear about what constitutes firm plans.

The confusion arises because females tend to apply the same "rules of having made firm plans" to males as we do with our female friends. Two female friends can make plans to get together on a certain day to do a certain activity together, and not have a firm time set. However, the plans are still considered firm. This is *not* the case in a male's world.

In the male mind, if a day, date, place, *and* time (all four) are not *all* ascertained, you two do not have firm plans/a date. If you two don't confirm all four of these details, the plans are not firm and do not exist in the male's mind. You have the *possibility* of plans/a date, but you don't have firm plans/a date.

Time and again, I hear frustrated females sharing stories about a male making mention of getting together on a certain day in the future. At that moment, in a female's mind, that day is now locked in. We have firm plans, she thinks. Leading up to the given day, she is awaiting his call or text to confirm the details, while putting on hold any other potential plans she may have for the day. It's now the "day of." She waits, calls, and texts and doesn't hear from him. She is pissed off and upset because in her mind, he's stood her up. "He disrespected my time," she thinks. Or he's playin' games. Newsflash: He hasn't stood you up, canceled on you, or disrespected your time. Why? Because in his mind, you two didn't have firm plans in the first place. One or two of the aspects of a date being firm were missing. This simple insight can spare you the confusion and frustration that is prevalent in the "dating scene," and bring clarity and peace of mind to your courtship experiences.

Keeping the energy units balanced

For most of us, this conversation about energy units is new and we haven't heard mention of this in the context of male/female interactions, dating, or courtship before. It follows that most of us have not given any deep thought to the notion of energy units (EUs). Interestingly, we can certainly sense when they're out of balance, but we don't know how to keep them in better balance. Courtship enables us to do this. I'm now going to use some simple math to illustrate the use of energy units to manage courtship and to show you how quickly energy becomes imbalanced in the modern dating paradigm.

Note: The lower end of the number of energy units is used in each example, for simplicity's sake and to avoid exaggerating the number of energy units. The math is based upon the time EUs being the same for the male and the female. The chart on page 97 shows how the EUs stack up between a typical dating scenario on the left and a modern courtship scenario on the right.

Energy Unit Conversion

$1.00	= 1 EU
Daytime minute	= 1 EU
Evening Minute	= 10 EU

First Date			
Typical Dating Scenario	*Energy Units*	*Courtship Scenario*	*Energy Units*
First Date - Evening	10 EUs	**First Date** - Daytime	1 EU
Dinner, two to three hours = 120 to 180 minutes.	120 EUs	Coffee, tea, or smoothies 1 hour = 60 minutes	60 EUs
Dinner cost, based upon having drinks or appetizers, and entrees, $100. Based upon the guy paying.	100 EUs	Coffee, tea, or smoothies, $10	10 EUs
EUs expended for Male, date #1	230 EUs (Male)	EUs expended for Male courtship date #1	71 EUs (Male)
EUs expended for Female (less the 100 money EUs), date #1	130 EUs (Female)	EUs expended for Female (less the 10 money EUs), courtship date #1	61 EUs (Female)
TOTAL EUs	**460 EUs**	**TOTAL EUs**	**132 EUs**
Male/Female EU difference from date #1	100 EUs	Male/Female EU difference from courtship date #1	10 EUs

Notice how many *more* energy units are involved in the typical dating scenario compared with the courtship scenario. By the end of the conventional date #1, a total of 460 EUs have been expended by both, while in the courtship dating scenario only 132 EUs have been expended by both. Also notice the difference in EUs between the female and male at the end of each scenario. The difference, or gap, in female/male EUs after typical date #1 is 100 EUs while in the courtship scenario it's only 10 EUs.

Remember, one of the objectives of cou rtship is to keep energy units as balanced as possible and to increase them *gradually*. As was mentioned earlier, the typical dating scenario creates significant imbalance in EUs even on the first date, compared with the courtship scenario.

When a minimal amount of energy units have been initially expended by both, it is much easier to respectfully transition to closure after a first date. Neither of you has to avoid or dodge the other, feel beholden to the other, feel guilty, or create lies or excuses if one or both of you is not interested in having another date. The more EUs that have been expended, the more awkward, difficult, or uncomfortable it can be to "back out" if it isn't working out. No

harm, no foul, no hard feelings. As you progress forward to subsequent outings you can gradually increase the amount of time and money expended,
gradually increasing EUs as you get to know each other: a day date for one
hour the first time, a day date for a couple of hours the second time, and then
continue to graduate, eventually to an evening get-together, for example.

When EUs are imbalanced. When there's an imbalance, both of you can
usually sense it, and the male often feels the imbalance more vividly because
he has more likely expended the most money energy units. Okay, so get ready
for an important and maybe even surprising insight.

One of the ways males sometimes seek to regain EU balance is with Goodness energy units, that is, through sex. The adage about men wanting only
"one thing" is usually the result of EUs being grossly out of balance, a female
not being a great date on top of it, and his being out of real money energy
units that he can't get back, whether you were a bad or a great date. He's out
of those dollars either way. But remember our earlier discussion about rushing to have sex too soon—we need to take responsibility for our participation
and stop casting men as "sex hounds," while casting ourselves as the "angelic
innocents" or victims when it comes to having sex too soon or too early on in
the series of interactions with a guy, though we've been obliging and partici-
pating all the way.

For many females the solution is to pay their own way (go Dutch) so that
the guy isn't seeking some Goodness at the end of the night. However, if you
align with and abide by the courtship principles, you can keep the energy
units balanced without having to go the route of going Dutch. It's your choice
and your prerogative, of course.

Exercise 9.3
Beginning To Make the Shift from Dating To Courtship

This may be the first you've heard of the notion of "Modern Courtship
Principles." Share what you learned from this discussion. _____
_____

If you're interested in shifting out of dating into courtship, list three changes
you're committed to making.

1. _____
2. _____
3. _____

Chapter Ten

Love Lie #8: He Should *Already* Know

⁂

*The He-Should-Already-Know (H.S.A.K.)
Syndrome exists against the backdrop
of the Expectations Love Lie and the A-Man-
Completes-Me Love Lie.*

⁂

Unless you've been detoxed of the Love Lies, you're probably operating from the insane, dysfunctional belief that he's supposed to make you happy: my happiness is his responsibility not mine; if he meets the requirements of my list, he is The One; and The One is supposed to automatically fulfill my expectations and meet my needs.

To further support this insanity, the H.S.A.K. Syndrome extends out of the beliefs that "he should already know what I think, how I think, what works for me, what doesn't work for me, what's important to me, and what I want him to do." I'm convinced that the H.S.A.K. Syndrome is one of the Love Lies that comes to us directly out of chick flick movies, romance novels, and romantic comedies. When a female operates from this Love Lie, she assumes he knows or *should* know what she likes or dislikes and wants him to know without her having to tell him. She erroneously believes that her having to tell him isn't as romantic or honorable, or that he cares about her less or doesn't truly love her. We usually apply the warped thinking of this Syndrome to our wants and desires, how we want to be touched or kissed, what he should stop doing, what he should start doing or do more of, or what irritates us, and for married women, what we think he should already know to do around the house.

If he doesn't *already* know, we surmise (1) it's not as important to him as it is to me, or (2) it's not important to him in the same way it is to me, or (3) he's wrong, insensitive, or doesn't care. In other words, if he really loves me, He Should Already Know. If he really cares about me, He Should Already Know. *None* of which is usually the case.

When the H.S.A.K. Love Lie is alive and well in you, the following thinking and behaviors usually accompany it:

- You think he should already know what you want him to do something, even though you haven't asked him or given details or clear instructions.
- You infer, assume, or drop hints, and expect him to "get" it though you have not been clear, direct, or explicit.
- You expect him to think the same way you do or see things the same way you do.
- You expect him to put the same weight and importance on what you put weight and importance on.
- You want him to think and react in the way a good female friend would think and react.
- You want him to do something the same way you would do something.
- You nag, complain, and/or make negative comments about the way he *is* doing something or because he's *not* doing something.

Operating from within the H.S.A.K. Syndrome yields problematic patterns in our relationships that are specific and consistent.

The result may be a closing down (closing down your heart and withdrawing or contracting your energy) for you because:

- you can incorrectly interpret his behavior as uncaring or unloving.
- you're frustrated because you think he's trying to be difficult.
- you may think he's being insensitive.
- you assume he "already knows" and thus isn't taking the desired or wanted action because he's choosing to be belligerent or defiant, or trying to irritate you on purpose.

The result for him may be withdrawal because:

- he feels frustrated.
- he feels "nit-picked."
- he feels inadequate.
- he feels as though, "No matter what I do, she's never satisfied."

The H.S.A.K. Syndrome is causing many of our frustrations and irritations, especially within marriages.

In the Love Academy, participants often ask, "Debrena, why should I have to *tell* him. Why should I have to *ask* him?" My response to them is, "Who told you 'not telling' and 'not asking' works with men? Where did you get this notion from? Why are you getting hung up on making a request (more on making requests later) or lovingly and clearly telling him, if it is the means to getting what you say you want? You certainly don't *have* to. You can continue being frustrated. It's your choice. It's about *what works* and what gets the results you want."

I've noticed that females consider making requests dishonorable or unromantic. I used to think this way, too. A crazy belief we're holding says, "If I have to make a request it's not as valid as if he did it himself or thought of it 'on his own'; or it means his action is not genuine." This is bogus! Ladies, in most cases in a love relationship or marriage: as a fact, he loves you, he cares about you, you're important to him, and he wants to please you. Here's the deal: Is it about getting what you want, or not? It's that simple. If it is about getting what you want, then ask so that your request can be fulfilled (or tell him, if that's what's fitting), to your liking. It's time to cut this Love Lie–riddled thinking off at the knees.

Love Truth #8
He Probably Doesn't Know

And with regard to relationships, what you're assuming he knows, or want him to know, or think he should know, most likely he doesn't know. So unless you learn to ask for what you want, you simply aren't going to be able to receive what you want in the way that works best for you, and you aren't going to experience satisfaction.

Even the things that are obvious to *us* in relationships are often not obvious to men. Have you noticed? And most likely the females he's encountered in his previous relationships were operating from this same Love Lie and didn't season him (more on this in Part 3), nor did she know how to communicate in Manese (more on this in Part 3 also). Unless a guy has been well-seasoned by previous women (not girls)—and *most males haven't*—he is in a raw, unseasoned state with regard to understanding women and relationships. In my Men-tality sessions, when I make this statement, men are willing to readily admit this.

Left to the devices of his social conditioning, the typical male has done his best to "piece together" his relationship knowledge and knowledge of women from overheard talk in the locker room, at the bar, or on the sidelines at the sports field, or from past experiences and/or failures. A very, very small percentage of males have actually been mentored by a mature male.

Getting your mindset ready to make requests

The good news is that this Love Lie is probably the easiest to recover from, if you're coachable and willing to accept some instruction. It will serve you well and make life easier for him. You can end this syndrome in your relationship or marriage by learning to make requests in Manese.

The H. S. A.K. is also rooted in our own gender conditioning. We have been taught to anticipate the needs of others, and if we can do it without them having to ask, even better. After all, *we're* expected to already know and anticipate others' needs. When it comes to our own needs and support, we are taught, usually by the behavior modeled by older females, including our mothers, to make subtle hints or be indirect. We sigh heavily and audibly to let others know that we'd appreciate some help, or we start slamming cabinets and cupboards louder, hoping they'll catch the hint. We make statements like "It sure would be nice if . . .," or our word choice seeks permission, or is tentative and meek, like "Would it be okay if . . ." or "Could I maybe . . ." So making requests in our love relationships is a very underdeveloped skill for most females, and something that has to be learned and practiced. For most of us, our "request muscles" need some serious development and strengthening.

I'm now going to teach you how to make a request in Manese to bring about a new, different, or better behavior in him, or if you have a personal desire, want, or preference that involves him. A request has a standard, simple, and clear structure. Instead of assuming, inferring, hoping, wishing, or dropping hints, you make it easier on both of you when you make a request.

Though this may sound simple enough, in Love Academy sessions we do live role-play practices to begin to get comfortable speaking Manese and making requests. It is amazing to see how much females struggle with formulating a request. I certainly understand. Learning to make requests required me to rethink my communication patterns within my relationship. I discovered that I was narrating, commentating, and giving directives, all the while *thinking* I was making a request and thinking I was being clear. Before I knew how to speak Manese, I was making statements in Womanese with lead-in phrases such as:

Why don't you . . .   Can't you . . .
It would be nice if you . . .   I want you to. . . .
I'd like you to . . .

None of these is a lead-in for a request.

For example, there was a time when I would say things to my husband like, "Having to cook dinner every night is too stressful after a full day of running my business. Sure would be nice if you helped out with dinner more," or "Sure would be nice if you helped out around the house more," all the while, *thinking* I was making a request. I would get irritated and upset because, in my mind, I was letting him know that I wanted help with dinner or around the house. In my mind, he was now supposed to heed my comment and start cooking dinner more regularly or kick into gear helping around the house more. Once I learned to speak Manese, I realized that my previous comments were in Womanese. I was being indirect and expected him to infer exactly what I meant, without having to be clear and explicit. For example, I converted this indirect comment into a request: "Honey, would you be responsible for taking care of dinner on Monday nights?" His response was yes, and he's been taking care of dinner on Monday nights ever since, whether he cooks dinner or brings home take-out.

In the Love Academy we actually practice making requests. And guess who struggles the *most* with making requests? *Married women!* I purposely choose a married woman for a role play with me, since making requests in our marriages is usually foreign to our communication pattern. Even after I give her the lead-in prompts for making a request, and a simple fill-in-the-blank example, it still takes several tries. Why? In our marriages especially, we're often narrating, commentating, or giving directives, but we're not making requests! Like clockwork, the married participant in the role plays throws up her hands in frustration after the fifth try and says, "So what do you want me to say? I don't get it!" That's when I bring them back to the simple structure of a request that I initially laid out. I explain it again. Usually the sixth try is the charm.

Remember: he wants to get it right. He wants to successfully fulfill your requests. Men are feat-oriented. They get tremendous satisfaction from successfully achieving deeds, tasks, or assignments. So fulfilling requests gives them satisfaction. And remember, if you are making a request that entails a new or different behavior for him, then you most likely will have to lovingly remind him or make the request again, when it's time.

As you prepare to learn how to make requests, here are some things to keep in mind about men and communication. When you make a request of a man:

- Be direct, clear, explicit, and literal. No inferring or assuming.
- Start the request with "Will you" or "Would you," followed by an action, and conclude with a question mark. Remember, Will you or Would you, not Can you. It's not about can he do it, or his capability. He's most likely physically and mentally capable. It's about will he or would he.
- Let go of the crazy notion that making a request diminishes the satisfaction of getting what you want or that it's less romantic or meaningful when it gets fulfilled.
- When he fulfills a request, does something that pleases you or works for you, *each time* (I repeat, each time), let him know immediately and directly. You can say, for example, "I really like it when . . . I love/loved it when . . . That was great when you. . . ."
- Be mindful of your body language, gestures, facial expressions, and especially your voice inflection. Men are highly attuned to our voice inflection. They can raise and lower the volume of their voices, but being able to inflect is one of our feminine gifts.

The "ingredients" of an effective request

Making requests is a muscle I've continued to strengthen in my relationship, and with tremendous results. Requests are a communication tool. Use requests in your relationship to get what you want, desire, prefer, or for assistance, help, or support. A request has a specific structure.

- It starts with *Would you* or *Will you* . . . not *Can you.*
- It contains a verb/action.
- It concludes with a question mark.
- It's specific.
- A yes or no response is required.

For example, after several years of date nights with my husband, I realized I wanted him to start opening and closing my car door for me, after years of me opening my own car door when we'd go out on dates. This was a new behavior. I wanted to bring about a new/different behavior, so I made a request: "Honey, when we go out on our date nights, will you open and close my car door for me from now on?" Of course he said yes. What's funny is that I was so used to opening and closing my own car door that *I* forgot on the next date night and got in and out of the car myself, like usual. I realized that I was undermining the very new behavior I wanted to call forth. So on our next date, I calmly and sweetly made the request to him again, and let him know I'd actually remember to *let* him open my car door this time. I had to refrain from the familiar pattern of opening and closing my own car door and instead wait for him to come around to my side of the car to open the door for me. We must remember that new behaviors that you want to see may require new behaviors on your part, too.

If he's able, has the time, and he's not angry with you, then his answer to your requests will usually be yes. There are times when you may get a no answer. I've found that this is usually due to poor timing or the timeline in which you might want the request fulfilled. If either of these don't work for a man, he'll say no to your request. When you're in your woman you realize that you may get a no once in a while, and you're okay with this. A request is not manipulation in disguise. Being okay with a no is what makes it a request in the first place. There's a reason there's a question mark at the end of the request. When a man answers no, treat it as a no *this time*. Release any "girl-ish" passive/aggressive tactics if you get a no once in a while. If you get a no response, he may have a counteroffer, you might re-state your request based upon a different timeline, or you can decide to make the request again in the future. It's certainly not the end of the world, nor is it likely a sign of rejection (so don't make it mean that in your mind).

Exercise 10.1
Manese Practice Makes Perfect

Let's say you'd like your husband to give you more nice, long hugs, like he used to when you were dating. (Though this particular example applies to married women, the general principles apply to single women.)

You might already have said something like one of the following:

1. It sure would be nice if you would give me nice, long hugs like you used to when we were dating.
2. You haven't given me one of those nice, long hugs in years.
3. I miss those nice, long hugs you used to give me when we were dating.
4. What happened to the nice, long hugs you used to give me?
5. You need to give me more hugs.

You may be surprised to know that *none* of these is a request. Each is instead one of the following:

1. an example of indirectly dropping a "back door" hint
2. a statement
3. commentary
4. an inquiry
5. a demand/directive

Now you give it a try: How would you restate this as a request? Refer back to the Elements of an Effective Request if you need to. Please rewrite it here:

_____

You can lead off with some "typical" female narration or commentary, but then *be sure to conclude by making the request.* The request is what makes the desired behavior you'd like from him plain and clear. And when he is clear about the actions you desire, it is much more likely that he will fulfill the request.

I'm probably doing a little overkill on this, but that's how big a difference it makes in a relationship. I want you to really understand how to make a request. So here are the elements of a full-blown request, using the hug example:

1. I miss those nice, long hugs you used to give me when we were dating. (This kind of lead-in commentary can be useful because it's giving him some useful data that he may not have been aware of.)
2. Now, follow up this commentary with your request: Would you + (action) give me + (be specific) at least two nice, long hugs a day?
3. To strengthen your request, you can also tell him *why* it matters to you. "I really like feeling your arms around me."

Now let's glue all of these pieces together: the commentary, the request, and why it matters to you.

"I miss those nice, long hugs you used to give me when we were dating. Would you give me at least two nice, long hugs a day? I really like feeling your strong arms around me." Now you await a response to this request.

Remember, if you get a no response, this may mean that he will still fulfill the request, but not on the timeline you offered. When you put forth a request, then you have to be sure to give the other person the latitude and respect to respond with either a yes or no.

Chapter Eleven

Love Lie # 9: I Can't Change a Man

———————— ❧ ————————

*I'm sure you've heard other women say it,
or maybe you've even said it yourself: You can't change
a man. I've watched numerous TV talk shows over the
years featuring love relationships experts, and before the
end of the show the expert usually utters the words: You
can't change a man. As the camera pans the audience,
usually made up of 95 percent women, the audience
members nod their heads in agreement.*

———————— ❧ ————————

We reach this conclusion because our attempts at trying to change a man have been frustrating and often fruitless, along with the majority of other females. But widespread agreement among females *doesn't* mean that it's true. When you're "in your girl," the way you attempt to get a man to change is through what amounts to nagging and complaining. Nagging and complaining wears on the male spirit, and over time can cause him to withdraw or become passive. He'd be happier listening to fingernails scratching across a chalkboard.

When we judge and assess men based upon an internal scorecard that consists of fixed, static features rather than internal, changing, and expanding qualities, we develop a false perception of men as static and fixed. This perception supports this Love Lie.

What's so interesting is that we've "bought" the You-Can't-Change-a-Man Love Lie, yet we keep trying to do it, and unsuccessfully, which then further reinforces the Love Lie. To a man's ears nagging and complaining may sound like, Why did you . . . Why don't you . . . Why couldn't you just . . . What were you thinking . . . You're doing it wrong . . . You never . . . . When we're operating from this lie we negatively comment on the behavior he's doing that we *don't* like, over and over again—it could be the toilet seat being left up, the cap being left off the toothpaste, clothes being left on the floor, or not checking in or being in better communication when you two are apart—and/or we constantly criticize and find fault with what he does.

What are you activating in a man?

The current Love Lies paradigm doesn't acknowledge that there is a broad range of potential qualities that reside within a man. This also is the case with you and every other human being. We have access to a full range of qualities, emotions, and responses internally. Within you (and me, too), at any given moment, there resides the potential for anger, joy, hatred, delight, happiness, pride, jealousy, sadness, sorrow, excitement, gratitude, and fear, to name a few. Different circumstances, people, and situations can invoke different qualities, emotions, and responses from within us. Have you noticed how you can spend time around a certain person, and they "bring out" the best in you, while you can spend time around another person and they "bring out" the worst in you? It's you in both situations, but what each is activating in you is different.

We encounter what we call "typical male behavior" and we conclude, "That's just the way men are." What we are actually experiencing or witnessing is the similar patterns of behavior from men that are emerging *in response* to what most females are activating in males and to the way most females are *being* in their interactions with men!

What circuits are you turning on in a man? Think of it like this: within him a man possesses a diverse array of "circuits" that are in the off position. Each of these circuits has the potential to be in the on position. Let's say these circuits are on a continuum. On the left end are those labeled "lower-quality circuits," qualities like selfish, aggressive, insensitive, domineering, egotistical, sneaky, and dishonest. On the right end of the continuum are the circuits labeled "high-quality circuits," qualities like generous, affectionate, thoughtful, disciplined, attentive, honest, or focused, for example.

When we're "in our girl," we tend to trigger the lower-quality circuits in males. These circuits are "flipped on" by "girl" energies and behaviors, such as neediness, nagging and complaining, heavy expectations, insecurity, low self-esteem, lack of self-love, distrust, unhealed emotional baggage, and looking to a man to save her, complete her, or bring her happiness. When we're in our girl, a state of being that is a by-product of the Love Lies, the corresponding behavior and qualities activated in a man can take the form of being domineering; controlling; emotionally explosive; abusive emotionally, mentally, or even physically; dishonest, unreliable, and untrustworthy; resigned or passive; manipulative; angry; frustrated; inflexible; or obstinate, to name a few.

You could also think of this phenomenon in terms of a piano metaphor. A standard piano has 88 keys. When a piano key is pressed, a hammer flies up inside the body of the piano and strikes the strings within the piano that correspond to that note. The note then produces an audible vibration. In this concept of activating certain qualities in a man, similarly, you are able to strike a key that then invokes a certain response, emotion, quality, or behavior in a man. The note he's "sounding" is in response to the "key" you're striking.

Different females can activate the same man differently. I first realized that different females activate different qualities and behaviors in the same man when I moved to Seattle at age 24. I grew up an hour south of Seattle, in Lacey, Washington, a much smaller, family-oriented town. Since I didn't attend high school in Seattle, I didn't have any personal previous history there. So Seattle, the big city, was like a whole new world to me. Within a few months of moving, I was dating several guys (having sex with none of them, by the way). One of these was Darren Corson (name changed), who was a former basketball star at our state's second largest university. One evening, a bunch of my new friends were sitting around my apartment gossiping about different Seattle guys. I was in the kitchen getting more snacks, but could overhear their conversation in the living room, discussing one particular guy. There was a consensus that this guy was stuck-up, insensitive, narcissistic, self-centered, and a "dog" to females. Each of them seemed to agree. They'd either had a personal experience with this particular guy or they knew a friend who had.

While I was listening and continuing to reload the appetizer tray, I thought to myself, "Whew, this guy sounds notorious for screwing women over." I then walked back into the living room with the snack tray reloaded and asked the name of the guy they were discussing. When they said Darren Corson, I almost choked on the wine I was sipping. Why was this so shocking to me? Because just the night before I had been sitting in Darren's apartment living room, on his couch, while he was in his kitchen making dinner for me. He brought my dinner out to me on a teakwood dinner tray, complete with stuffed lobster, drawn butter, steamed asparagus, a glass of white wine, a single rose in a bud vase, and even an after-dinner mint! He was attentive, caring, generous, and respectful. By the time we finished eating dinner and talking, I was starting to fall asleep. He offered me his bed, while he slept on his couch, so that I wouldn't have to drive home so late. I graciously accepted his offer, on the condition that he wasn't going to try and slip into the bed with me during the night to get some Goodness. He assured me that he wouldn't, and he kept his word. When I left early the next morning, he insisted on me waking him up so that he could see me to the door. He was a consummate gentleman. The Darren I had experienced the night before sounded like a completely different Darren from the one they were describing—and he was. Clearly, what I was activating in him was very different from what other females were consistently activating in him.

In that moment, I realized that a different female can activate the same man differently. What is creating this misperception that you can't change a man? Could it be that, collectively, most of us are "in our girl," and thus we are activating the same types of qualities, striking the same keys, flipping on the same circuits in men, and invoking similar responses in men? The answer is yes.

Love Truth #9
Oh, Yes, I Can Change a Man!

When a female is "in her woman" (not in her girl), she is conscious of and recognizes the fact that she can affect change in a man. In other words, she recognizes that she has the power and the ability to cause certain circuits to flip from off to on, thus activating certain qualities and behaviors that already exist within him.

I recently came across a scientific research study that blew my mind, and also confirmed this phenomenon of a woman being an "activator." Even at the molecular level, in the dynamics between the egg and the sperm, we see evidence of this phenomenon. Scientists have known for years that the sex hormone progesterone is released from ovulated eggs, and it helps the sperm identify and navigate toward the egg. What two studies have recently discovered is *how* this actually happens: the progesterone hormone released by the egg actually *activates* calcium ion transporters found in the tail of the sperm.

It's these calcium ion transporters that make the sperm's tail undulate back and forth faster.

Just as the egg (the female principle) activates the sperm (the male principle) with the progesterone hormone emitted by the egg, a woman is able to activate certain qualities in a man.

The notion of trying to find The One, based in the I-Have-a-Sole-Soul-Mate and Requirements List Love Lies, reveals that we consider a man to be fixed, static, and unchanging. We operate as if a "Good Man" is a prepackaged item you can find at your grocery store. Since there are many possibilities within him, we're interested in activating and attracting the good *in* a man. Yes, there will continue to be males out there who exhibit despicable, disrespectful behavior and continue to act from their lower qualities, activated by other people or by their environment; however, the notion I'd like you to consider here is that it's about being able to activate the good in a man.

I bring this up not for you to run out and look for men who can be your fix-up projects but because I want you to recognize that your beliefs, your behaviors, your energy and presence, and your ways of engaging men invoke certain and very specific responses. You are a powerful force. You have something to do with how a man is behaving in response to you—you're that powerful. If you are consistently activating a man's lower circuits or his lower qualities, then this is especially important feedback you need to heed. This gives you the opportunity to develop and refine certain qualities within yourself. Increase your own vibration and upgrade your beliefs and behaviors so that you can activate higher qualities or higher vibrations within a man.

I want to draw your attention to your presence, the energy you bring, your bilingual abilities, the responses you invoke, and your ability to activate certain responses or behaviors. These are *all* ways in which you effect change in a man. Now we understand why a man can be one way with one woman and a completely different way with another—he is not the *same* man, so to speak. Each woman is invoking different qualities from within him.

Nancy's story

Nancy, age 33, participated in Love Academy 101 and 201. She came to the course in the fifth year of her second marriage, having been married previously for six years to her former husband. She was noticing the same types of patterns starting to emerge in her current marriage that had emerged in her first marriage, and she wanted to avoid going down the same road. Nancy describes her "before and after" experience.

Prior to Love Academy, I was "in my girl." I was demanding, over-controlling, and I was not leading from a feminine space at all. In my previous marriage, and in my current one, up until taking the Love Academy, I thought that I had to do everything and if I didn't do it, it wouldn't get done. I operated from a martyr type of behavior and wouldn't accept help. But refusing help led me to feeling resentful.

With both my previous and current husband, I made them feel as though they could never get anything right. I would invalidate what they were saying, over-talk them, cut them off in midsentence, nag and complain, and insist that my way was the better way. My responses would be laced with sarcasm and irritation. Eventually they would say "Never mind," at some point, or some version of "I'm just going to stay the hell out of your way!"

Love Academy taught me two particularly pivotal things: I am the natural leader in my relationship and I am an activator. What I was successful at activating in my former and current husband was anger, withdrawal, and disengagement. Two different men, same pattern, because my behavior was the same.

Now I realize that I can choose to activate different behaviors in my current husband, now that I understand what's really going on. I started listening and not cutting him off, being soft, flowing, and being even softer and sweeter with my voice, opening my heart to him, and believing and knowing that his thoughts and ideas are important to me. I now make requests. I no longer believe in trying to do it all myself. I ask for help, and I am able to receive it. I am absolutely amazed at the shift I am witnessing in my husband as I've begun to shift and detox from this Love Lie. My husband is more engaged, more receptive, he hugs and kisses me more around the house, seeks out my advice and perspective now, initiates sex more, and is helping out around the house more.

On one of my Love Academy trips, I had the chance to meet Nancy's husband, Jason, in person. He gave me a huge hug and said, "Debrena, I don't know what you've done to my wife, but I love it. She's now a completely different person in our marriage. She's a new woman! Thank you!"

Exercise 11.1
Being an Activator

Step 1 (look at your past):

1. What behaviors and emotions have I been *activating* in men (in the past)?

_____

_____

_____

2. In the past, what specific qualities most often showed themselves when I was engaging with men? _____

_____

_____

Step 2 (look at your present and future):

1. What qualities and behaviors am I noticing that I activate right now, with men?

_____

_____

_____

2. What qualities and behaviors do I desire to activate in a man going forward (in the future)? _____

_____

_____

Are your answers between the two questions in step 1 the same or different? Are your answers between the two questions in step 2 the same or different? Is there a gap? For most of us, there is a gap between what's been showing up and presenting itself in our past or present, and what we desire to have show up and present itself now. *When what we're activating is out of alignment with what we desire to activate in a man, we have a gap.*

Step 3: Review the qualities and behaviors you listed in question #2 in step 2. If there's a gap between the qualities and behaviors that have been showing up and what you want to have show up, this lets you know that there's some divine self-work to do. Identify what the gap reveals as the qualities you need to grow and develop within yourself or behaviors that you want to change. For example, you may notice that you're activating flakiness or dishonesty, but desire to activate consistency and honesty. This gap reveals that, within yourself, you might want to work on operating with more integrity and consistency or putting aside your masks and learning to be more real.

List those areas you want to work on to close the gaps here.

1. _____
   _____
2. _____
   _____
3. _____
   _____
4. _____
   _____
5. _____
   _____

Chapter Twelve

Love Lie #10: I Am the Follower

In the context of relationships I refer to "follower"
as a mindset in which a female sees herself as "less than,"
inferior to a male, behind or below him, secondary,
or of lesser importance or significance.

This Love Lie is particularly fueled by the A-Man-Completes-Me, Self-Love-Is-Optional, and I-Have-a-Sole-Soul-Mate Love Lies, all of which infer that the male is superior, the one to seek and find, or the one she hopes to be chosen by, saved by, or completed by.

By the way, this is the Love Lie I was most reluctant to include in this book. I anticipated it could be controversial because it challenges the prevailing hierarchical mindset about marriage and discusses the concept of feminine leadership in love relationships and marriage. However, it became increasingly clear that I was supposed to include it in this book. What I'm about to share may seem contrary to much of what you've been told and taught to believe, but I ask you to keep an open mind.

When a female is operating from the I-Am-the-Follower Love Lie in her relationships, it can show up in many unhealthy ways: ignoring her intuition and inner wisdom; having sex too soon or consenting though, internally, it's not what she really wants to do; staying in unhealthy or toxic relationships for too long; tolerating disrespectful treatment or behavior; returning to a man repeatedly though he has shown that he is abusive or can't be trusted; becoming overly compliant; silencing or suppressing her voice; getting resigned or passive; or foregoing what she wants in the name of compromise.

The I-Am-the-Follower Love Lie misleads you into believing it's the man who is initiating and establishing the tone and tempo in a relationship, and the female who is responding. This may *appear* to be what's happening, but in actuality the female is leading, *whether consciously or unconsciously*, with her words, gestures, nonverbal communication, and energy, and with what she tolerates or allows. The male is responding moment to moment. When a female buys into this Love Lie, she doesn't realize that she sets the tone and the "keynote" that prevails in the relationship.

We, at first, may think that feminine leadership contradicts the notion of male headship in covenant marriage, but it doesn't. It actually enhances it, as you will see. We can be further challenged by the concept of females as the natural leaders in relationships because we haven't seen living examples of feminine leadership within the domain of love relationships. Even the females depicted on TV and in the movies are operating "in their girl" in their relationships, which disqualifies them from effective and mature leadership in their relationships.

Love lie #10 in the covenant marriage

In my personal coaching work, especially when working with Christian married women, I've noticed a disturbing trend among wives: they feel both resentful and disempowered. When a female is operating from the I-Am-the-Follower Love Lie in her marriage, she can erroneously believe that "being a good wife" is about denying her power and her voice, and considering hers less important than her husband's. She can suppress her full self-expression, silence her voice out of frustration, continually subjugate herself to control or manipulation, or be plagued with inner discontent, despite the smile she may have plastered on her face. She can buy into a warped notion of compromise in which she foregoes what she considers to be important in the name of love, or she buys into faulty messaging that erroneously associates love with sacrifice, and sacrifice as loss—her loss.

Similarly, many husbands have mistakenly been taught to interpret headship in marriage as hierarchical, ruling over, dominating, controlling, or demanding that "what I say goes." However, when there is disregard or devaluing of the perspective, gifts, advice, voice, or feedback of his spiritual partner, his wife, the result is not a partnership but a monarchy.

Whether you are Christian or non-Christian, you're probably aware of the influence of covenant marriage as it's presented in the Bible. For example,

"Til death do us part," a frequently recited line in both religious and secular marriage vows, is a remnant of more robust vows that clearly refer to the biblical stance on marriage as a spiritual covenant. Though love is the divine energy in love relationships, the Love Lies paradigm has eliminated the spiritual component of love relationships, and conveniently ignores the critical fact that a union of two spirits is occurring, in addition to a union of bodies, beyond the joining of bank accounts and material possessions. In this book, covenant marriage is recognized as a lifelong partnership in which the assignments of husband and wife have been divinely and precisely crafted so that there is an inherent balance of power, and the highest form of union and interdependence that can be experienced between a man and woman. The distinctive elements that set covenant marriage apart from cohabitation, and distinguish it from being only a legal entity, is the acknowledgement of covenant marriage as a lifelong spiritual union that establishes a sacred crucible in which husband and wife become increasingly aware of their divine nature, grow and develop together spiritually, and glorify God throughout their marriage journey. In particular, covenant marriage provides us the opportunity to learn to walk in the divine assignments of husband-headship and wife-leadership. So I'm now going to turn our attention specifically to covenant marriage for a few moments.

Moving beyond roles. The I-Am-the-Follower Love Lie can also cast the female as a passive follower and suppress the unique, necessary, and distinct contributions of feminine leadership within the covenant marriage. In the prevailing structure of marriage as we've understood it, having clear roles is typically lauded as being one of the keys to a functional marriage. However, I want to challenge this belief. Contributing to the misunderstandings regarding husband-headship has to do with headship being treated as a role instead of as a divine assignment with a special purpose. Roles may be the key to a standard, typical marriage, but I am interested in an atypical marriage—one that is deeply satisfying and fulfilling, where both partners are fully self-expressed. Roles work well in a theater production or on a TV or movie set, but not if we want to experience a *juicy* marriage in which both partners are actualized—one where there is satisfaction, fulfillment, and deep connection.

Roles, as we tend to fill them in the current paradigm, can be fixed and predetermined; roles can suppress self-expression and dictate how we're *supposed* to act and behave. However, understanding the divine assignments of husband

and wife is much more expansive and less constricting. The gifts of each person are based on their natural affinities and what they are best or better equipped to fulfill in the divine partnership of covenant marriage

In *The Marriage Spirit*, Drs. Evelyn and Paul Moschetta, a husband and wife counseling team, explain, "Historically, marriages were based on rigid, socially prescribed roles and expectations." Although roles have loosened and become more 50/50, the Moschettas assert something is still missing. I agree. "Couples yearn for a deeper kind of togetherness, a soul-centered love where there is a harmony of body, mind, and spirit, and the marriage has become a powerful vehicle for personal growth and self-transcendence." "You are spiritually intimate because you open your hearts to see and touch the divine in each other," the Moschettas explain, "and there is a free and effortless willingness to give and receive unselfish love." We yearn for spiritual intimacy. Our souls yearn for deep satisfaction and fulfillment, and fuller self-expression, where we are willing to shed the notion of roles as prescribed "relationship job titles."

Do Christian marriages fare better? As much as I want to be able to say that Christian marriages are exempt from the Love Lies, or are faring better than non-Christian marriages, I'm not able to. Unfortunately, the 51 percent divorce rate among Christian marriages matches that of secular marriages. Christian marriages are doing no better when it comes to the rate of divorce. I know— this can be a hard pill to swallow. As a Christian, it grieves my heart to have to acknowledge that Christian marriages are faring no better. We don't want to believe that Christian marriages are suffering equally from the Love Lies, are just as susceptible to them, and are no less infected by them. We want to believe that having a religious foundation trumps the messaging and influences of our cultural conditioning. We want to believe that Christians have figured out what it means to be doing marriage God's way. We must remember, however, that the Love Lies are instilled at a very young age—prior to starting to attend church in many cases, prior to having a firm grasp of biblical teachings, and before making a conscious salvation decision. So the Love Lies are alive and well in Christian marriages, too.

Could it be that there are some key biblical misinterpretations of covenant marriage that contribute to toxic relationship dynamics and have a majority of Christian marriages failing also? Are there misunderstandings about spiritual partnership and the divine assignments and functions of husband and wife that contribute to Christian marriages, *as we currently engage in them,* failing at the same rate as secular marriages? My experience and observations over the years through my teachings, training, and courses is that the answer to both is yes.

Headship and leadership in covenant marriage. The interpretation of the creation story has conditioned us to believe that since woman was created second, she's inferior to man and the passive follower. With woman being the apex of creation and the last and final version of human being, we know this to be a long-standing falsehood.

Traditionally, the interpretation of the divine assignments of husband and wife have acknowledged the headship of the husband and have excluded, whether intentionally or due to ignorance, the divine assignment of the feminine leadership of the wife. The reality of feminine leadership is a critical element that has been missing in our interpretation of scripture and thus has affected our understanding of marriage. Its absence in mention, teaching, and thus practice has both diminished and handicapped our ability to achieve and experience spiritual partnership in Christian marriages.

The prevailing interpretation of Christian marriage depicts headship and leadership as one and the same, as interchangeable, as synonyms, and as though they collapse into *one* function that is filled by the husband. Au contraire! *This misunderstanding of the headship function, and thus its misapplication, has perpetuated major misunderstandings of biblical teachings about covenant marriage, has created tremendous imbalance and confusion in general, and specifically, has done extensive damage within marriages.*

I'm suggesting that the equally high failure of Christian marriages is *not* because marriage, as it is designed by God and defined in the Bible, doesn't work, but because we are operating from partial, inaccurate, and dangerous misinterpretations of scripture that establish a false and faulty belief in male superiority and female subordination as condoned by God, when this is far from the truth.

In his book, *A Call to Action: Women, Religion, Violence and Power* former United States President Jimmy Carter describes how the "sustained religious suppression of women as inferior" contradicts the gospel's message of radical equality of human value, and suggests that it's been used "in depriving women of equal status within the worldwide secular community." I wholeheartedly agree.

Exercise 12.1
Reflections on Feminine Leadership

This is an opportunity to reflect on the widely accepted beliefs this Love Lie challenges. What are some new considerations about feminine leadership this section has illuminated for you? _____

_____

_____

_____

_____

Love Truth #10
I Am the Natural Leader and the Leader Naturally

As we discuss feminine leadership within relationships and the marriage covenant relationship, I caution you to avoid back-referencing other forms of leadership with which you may be familiar—leadership in the corporate world or the workplace, on the athletic field or court, or in the military. These are the forms and styles of leadership that we're most familiar with, but they do not apply here. We tend to be unfamiliar with feminine leadership in demonstration and practice, in the domain of the covenant marriage, so it's easy to get confused by these other models.

Feminine leadership, a term that conveys the unique female leadership qualities within relationships, has many forms of expression. Feminine leadership is rooted in our ability to influence decisions, the mood, and the emotional climate in our relationship with our feminine energy, and our gifts of intuition, openness, graciousness, listening, situational sensitivities, and a perspective that enables us to notice and observe nuances a man may miss. As mentioned previously, it means recognizing, for one, that men are constantly responding, moment by moment, to our feminine cues—our facial expressions, voice inflection, body language, gestures, our radiance, our energy and attitude, and what we allow and don't allow. We set the tone and tempo of relationships.

When we attempt to lead from our "girl," it manifests as criticizing, harshly judging, micromanaging, controlling, or operating from a place of basic distrust of men. Not a pretty sight. Feminine leadership is in its fullness when you're being "in your woman," knowing that you're the gift, leading from a place of maturity, and honoring your husband's headship.

As I explained earlier, the sperm *responds* to the sex hormone progesterone, released from the female's ovulated eggs. This hormone provides the chemical stimulus that helps the sperm identify and navigate toward the egg. Even at this level, we can see that the egg is leading, and the sperm is responding to its signals. This same type of phenomenon occurs within covenant marriage. The woman is initiating at very subtle ways within her relationship, and the man is responding. This is also the basis of what occurs in modern courtship. Wow!

Feminine leadership in covenant marriage

In Genesis 2:18-20, when it speaks of woman's creation in relation to man, it uses the term "suitable" to describe woman in relation to man. In this context, suitable means having matching, fitting, equal, or appropriate qualities. Contrary to popular interpretation, or more accurately, misinterpretation, hierarchy is not part of covenant marriage. Headship and leadership are distinct functions with distinct purposes that work in harmony, and alongside each other in the divine partnership of covenant marriage.

The first demonstration of feminine leadership is in the biblical creation story. As the story goes, Adam received a direct command from God not to eat from a certain tree in the Garden of Eden, the Tree of Knowledge. When Adam received this direct instruction, Eve had not yet been created and thus was not privy to receiving the instruction directly from God. However, in the book of Genesis, it is clear that Eve was aware of this command, so this instruction apparently was conveyed to her via Adam. In that moment, when Adam partook of the "forbidden fruit," the influence of Eve prevailed. She gave the fruit to him, and he ate it. In that moment, Eve's influence prevailed, even over God's instruction. It was the first demonstration of feminine leadership in action.

This was a powerful nuance of the creation story I had missed before. I'd never heard this pointed out in interpretations of the Garden of Eden story I'd heard in church coming from the pulpit over the years. The first example of woman's influence in action gets overshadowed by Eve being cast as the villain, and allegedly causing the downfall of humanity, though *both* Adam and Eve exercised their free will and were disobedient.

I bring up this biblical scenario, not to argue about *what* she influenced him to do (I am not condoning disobedience), but most important, to acknowledge this demonstration of her influence. Influence is one of the most important forms and expressions of feminine leadership, and thus one of the most easily abused. This is why we must be careful not to misapply this gift of influence for negative purposes, foul play, or manipulation. There are seriously negative consequences when this occurs.

I mentioned earlier how this particular Love Lie and its corresponding Love Truth were the hardest for me to include in this book. I actually tried to get out of it several times with God because I knew they were the most potentially controversial, but He wasn't having it. Interestingly, while in the midst of writing this particular section of the manuscript, I came across a used bookstore in the Raleigh, North Carolina, airport, on a return trip from leading a Love Academy 201 Advanced Course in Raleigh. I'm especially fond of used bookstores because they hold treasures of rare books, books no longer in print, or books written 40, 50, or 100+ years ago, containing wisdom that you can't find in contemporary books. This was my first time, however, encountering a used bookstore in an airport.

As I was perusing the bookshelves, I came across a book called *Woman to Woman: A Classic Inspirational Guide to Coping with Today's Complex World* by Eugenia Price. Well, wouldn't you know it—on page three of this book the author makes the comment, "God created into woman a particular power to influence," and cites Eve's influence with Adam in the Garden of Eden. Price goes on to add, "I am convinced that most women are not aware of the power of this innate ability to mark the lives of those whose lives we touch." It sounded like the author was a progressive, leading-edge contemporary, so I was bowled over when I saw that this book was published more than 50 years ago, in 1959!

What were the odds of coming across this particular book in a used bookstore at the airport, and deciding to buy it and read it during the very time I was working on the portion of my manuscript dealing with influence and feminine leadership? To me, this was divine intervention.

I agree with Price. The power of influence is not a power to be taken lightly, or to be misused or abused. The results can be ugly, toxic, or even deadly. This is why I continue to insist that we must mature from girl to woman so that we are productive and responsible with this power of influence; otherwise, we can scar ourselves and the hearts, souls, and lives of those around us.

Below is a list of verbs and simple descriptions I've assigned to the function of feminine leadership within the covenant marriage relationship. In action, practice, and demonstration, feminine leadership has many forms of expression, and may look like any of the following:

Visioning	Nudging	Intuiting
Anticipating	Planning	Yielding
Generating Ideas	Preparing	Encouraging
Suggesting	Fostering	Facilitating
Receiving Graciously	Listening Well	

In covenant marriage, headship and leadership are to be understood, not in isolation, but in the context of them interacting together. This is where the magic is. Below, I've presented you with some analogies and metaphors compiled from life, science, nature, and the Holy Bible, as well as "spiritual insights" I was given to further understand and communicate the interplay and the dynamics of headship and leadership. Remember, these are *not* absolutes, but are to begin to acquaint you with the interplay of the divine assignments.

The Dynamics of Masculine Headship	The Dynamics of Feminine Leadership
Pilot	Radar
Head	Heart
Giver	Receiver
Electricity	Conductor
Seed	Soil
The wheel of the "relation-ship"	The rudder of the "relation-ship"
Periscope	Binoculars
Mission	Vision

Understanding the nuances

The nuances and differences between headship and leadership in covenant marriage are numerous. The wife's natural feminine leadership in marriage can be expressed in many forms: making suggestions, using her influence to nudge and prompt her husband in a certain direction, raising a point for consideration, illuminating a perspective that has eluded him, influencing him toward a certain course of action, or using her touch or emotions to influence him.

The wife's natural feminine leadership is also expressed in her ability to anticipate future potential outcomes, and offer up considerations and alternatives from this perspective; her ability to envision and see the bigger picture for her marriage or her family; have a highly attuned "gut-level" response; provide an intuitive read on situations; offer recommendations and suggestions that reflect her feminine sensitivity; offer more inclusive approaches; suggest approaches that take the impact and consequence of actions into greater consideration; attention to detail; attention to time; attention to other's feelings; careful planning; thinking ahead; asking questions that ensure clarity about the situation; and initiating ideas that expand thinking or consider the new or the different.

Husband-headship calls for the husband keeping the partnership's best interests in mind and at heart; having a commitment to his wife being healthy in mind, body, and spirit; and loving her with a self-giving, cherishing, and generous love that nourishes her heart and her feminine spirit.

Husband-headship also consists of spiritual headship, wise decision-making, accountability, and a way of loving his wife in thought, word, and action that is consistent with considering her a precious gift. Masculine headship entails the husband having concern about the spiritual well-being of his wife and for the partnership (this includes husbands praying with and over their wives); considering her perspective and input; making wise decisions that are significant to the well-being and integrity of the marriage; being accountable for the decisions, behaviors, and choices of himself *as well as* his wife (this is an aspect of the husband-headship function of which many of us are unaware); and loving her as he would his own body.

Exercise 12.2
An Affirmation

In this exercise, an affirmation is provided that you can recite out loud, to yourself, or write down in your journal to be reminded of the honor and privilege of being given the natural leadership gifts of a woman. An affirmation is a positive, present tense, declarative statement that you desire to "make firm" in your thinking and eventually in your choices and behaviors. Personally, I've found that saying affirmations at the beginning and end of the day is especially powerful—in the morning as you're getting ready for a new day, and at night before you go to sleep so that these positive, affirming words are the last thing taken in to your mind before going to sleep.

Today, I look within and see my feminine leadership gifts in abundance.
Today, I appreciate being a woman, feeling and perceiving as a woman,
and leading as a woman.
Today, I graciously and readily offer and contribute my natural
feminine leadership gifts, in service, in a meaningful way.

Let the Detoxing Begin!

Chapter Thirteen

Introduction to the B.L.I.S.S.S. Healing & Awareness Program

Thus far, we've explained the origin and fall-out of the Love Lies, exposed the first 10 female Love Lies, and introduced their companion Love Truths. Now it's time to prepare you to move into the final section of this book—where you get to really roll up your sleeves and enter into the detox process.

This final section, Let the Detox Begin!, enters you into the six-part B.L.I.S.S.S. Healing & Awareness Program. This final part of the book facilitates further healing from the damage and "infection" of the Love Lies, builds and strengthens your new love relationship muscles and skills, and facilitates making the shift from girl to woman. It provides you with the opportunity to practice and apply the Love Truths in your thinking, behavior, and ways of relating to and engaging with men.

Now that you've been introduced to the Love Lies and the Love Truths, and have begun to awaken to a new way of seeing yourself, seeing men, and relating to and engaging in relationships, it's time to move into the detox phase of this journey. You're now in the final stretch. This is where you want to get your second wind and be sure to finish strong.

This is the perfect time to team up with friends who have read this book to be accountability partners through Part 3 of the awareness-raising and more intensive exercise-based section of the book.

This six-part program is the infrastructure of the detox process. The exercises contained in this section are based upon the very exercises I personally moved through and completed as part of my own divinely prescribed "growing up" process. They are not based upon theory or conjecture but have been tried and tested in the crucible of my own life as well as in the lives of hundreds of other women.

The detox process introduced in this section of the book is designed to (1) clean out and clear out blockages, (2) help the Love Truths become real for you and take root in you, (3) further strengthen your new relationship muscles, and (4) renew and recalibrate your believing, thinking, and ways of engaging with men such that deep satisfaction and fulfillment can be your reality instead of a pipe dream.

Remember, practice is what anchors these new teachings and principles within you, and in your life. Practice is about applying what's been shared here. It's "where the rubber meets the road."

Part 3, the B.L.I.S.S.S. Healing & Awareness Program enables you to:

- make the shift from being "in your girl" to being "in your woman,"
- let go of and replace old relationship beliefs,
- invoke your divine function of leadership as a woman,
- upgrade your communication skills so that you are bilingual (able to speak and understand Manese), and
- learn how to be a good "Man Seasoner,"
- experience a forgiveness process that actively heals your thoughts and emotions, supports you in re-opening your heart, and cleans out emotional residue and baggage from your past or current relationships, and
- access the power of sacred self-care in your life.

Be aware that a detox process can trigger a detox reaction as you move out of old beliefs, attachments, and behaviors. You may find yourself feeling challenged and stretched at times. You may think to yourself, "Whew, this is too much work." Yes, it takes work, divine self-work, and a willingness to take off the masks that the Love Lies can plaster to our faces. You can do it. You're worth it. Each interactive and experiential exercise included here is necessary, so I invite you do them thoroughly and completely.

Now, as you move through your daily life, your level of observation about the presence of Love Lies messaging in our culture should be elevated and heightened. Notice the behaviors and conversations of others going on around you that arise out of the Love Lies. This includes dialogue on TV, messaging that is presented via traditional and social media, and your own thoughts, behaviors, and inner self-talk. Once you've been exposed to something that expands your consciousness, questions your previous perceptions, changes your thinking, or awakens you, your awareness is heightened and you begin to notice things that previously went unnoticed. You will probably be surprised at what previously had been "flying under your radar." Instead of being in a fog or blindly accepting what you are seeing and hearing, noticing anew supports you in challenging your beliefs and changing your mind. This is what personal transformation is all about. This heightened awareness also indicates that you're awakening out of the Love Lies "auto-pilot" trance.

Here is a synopsis of the detox process, the six steps of the B.L.I.S.S.S. Healing & Awareness Program:

B = Be in Your Woman

Intimately acquaint yourself with the specific ways of being and behaving that characterize being "in your woman" versus being "in your girl." Begin to make the shift in tangible ways in your believing, thinking, and behavior.

L = Let Go of Old Beliefs

Unearth and dig up the faulty, disabling beliefs that are holding you hostage to your past. Release your grip on old beliefs and step into a set of new relationship beliefs that are liberating and empowering.

I = Invoke Your Feminine Leadership

Acknowledge and positively express your natural feminine leadership gifts in your current or future relationship(s) through the power of sacred self-care.

S = Stop the Communication Insanity

End the insanity cycle and upgrade your communication skills by becoming bilingual, being able to speak and understand Manese. Receive strategies for recovering from communication short circuits and restore the connection and flow of communication in your relationship(s).

S = Strengthen Your "Man Seasoning" Skills

Shares the steps to strengthening your "man seasoning" skills, including how to make and use requests to bring about positive change, employ the art of "speaking appreciation" to strengthen a man's spirit, and how to use the T.E.L.L. Him approach to increase desired behaviors that enrich the quality of the experience in your relationship.

S = Seek Healing and Forgiveness

The final step in the detox takes you through a comprehensive five-part forgiveness process, with a special focus on forgiving one's parents, in which you'll have the opportunity to begin unloading old baggage, blockages, and wounds in the form of hurt, pain, and unforgiveness from your past.

To look at my marriage years before my detox process, is to see a list of complaints and frustrations. I wanted to go deeper, I wanted to go higher, and I wanted more. I didn't want our marriage to slip into the ruts of complacency, living like roommates, stuck in routines and taking each other for granted, with no passion or vibrancy. After year 10, I was clear that I wanted him to initiate more physical touch. I wanted him to suggest and initiate date nights instead of me always being the one to bring it up. I had grown spiritually in my prayer and meditation life, and I wanted us to grow together spiritually. I wanted more quality connection time in our lives each week, where we could talk and share, and have some quality, bonding moments together a few times each week before going to bed, without any other distractions.

Before my detox process, I was convinced that my husband was the *entire* problem. After all, we had both committed to ending our outside sexual relationships a few years prior, and as I was to discover, he had continued to violate this agreement. In my mind, he was the one who needed to get his *sh*** together. I already had mine together, *so I thought*. In my mind and heart at that time, before detoxing, I truly believed that all would be well and fine in our relationship if my husband stopped screwing around (literally); if he did what I wanted him to do when and how I wanted him to do it; and fulfilled *my* expectations. It was his job to make me happy (so I thought at the time) and, in my eyes, he was falling short.

The transformation in my marriage happened in conjunction with my personal transformation, and my personal transformation happened in conjunction with my detox process. So instead of waiting for him to change, and believing that he was the one "at fault," I shifted. As mentioned previously, I discovered that *when I shift, he shifts, and when I shift, the relationship is shifted.*

Now he is highly affectionate at home and when we go out; he initiates dates more frequently; we (our family) now attend church together; the two of us pray together a few times a week out loud before we go to bed; he initiates sex more frequently; he is more responsive to my suggestions and advice; he gives me more compliments; he's more affectionate and generous with his compliments; and he has taken on more of the chores. He now pays closer attention and notices the special touches I like—a certain kind of clover honey for my fresh-squeezed lemon tea; preparing brunch on Sundays after church with his creamy grits or famous smothered potatoes; a kiss and hug before he leaves for work before the break of dawn each morning while I'm still asleep, etc. I now feel completely cherished, appreciated, and adored. *And it feels soooo deliciously good!*

Thanks to the detox process God revealed to me and led me though, and because I was (eventually) willing to accept *my* part in our marital problems, everything has changed. I feel and know that we now have a deeper, heart-to-heart connection, and a new and stronger foundation of trust that has our hearts opening wider and wider to each other. If this is what you want for yourself and your current or future relationships, then get ready to roll up your sleeves, engage in the B.L.I.S.S.S. Healing & Awareness Program, and do the divine self-work that will begin to decontaminate and detox you of the Love Lies.

Chapter Fourteen

B = Be in Your Woman
Making the Shift from Girl to Woman

---

*A quote from Simone de Beauvoir, French writer
and philosopher, captures it best when she says,
"One is not born a woman, one becomes one." This first
step in the B.L.I.S.S.S. Healing & Awareness Program is
to help usher you into being "in your woman."*

This is a shift that takes place on several levels—emotionally, mentally, spiritually, and "communicationally." Left to the devices of the Love Lies social conditioning, however, you will remain "parked" and stuck in girl. In my experience, making this shift is *an essential prerequisite* to the Love Truths "taking root" and becoming real in your life. Deep satisfaction and fulfillment will continue to elude you when you're operating in your girl. You must *consciously decide* to step into being in your woman, and then, only then, does deep satisfaction and fulfillment become a possibility for you.

Being in your girl versus being in your woman
Let's start with a Girl/Woman Overview:

1. A girl pouts and uses the silent treatment on a man when she gets upset. When she is angry, she closes down and broods or sulks. She is on the search to find The Only One that can "make" her happy, the one who scores the highest on her internal scorecard or for whom it appears that she can check off the most items on her Requirements List. She projects expectations onto men, emits an energy of neediness, and her radiance is very low.

2. A woman responds instead of reacts, and is able to speak and comprehend both Womanese and Manese. She recognizes that there are many soul mate possibilities that may exist, and she is relaxed and at ease about being able to attract men. Her radiance is on, and her glow is apparent. She cultivates within herself the qualities that she wants to attract, and attracts them, instead of buying into the illusion that a list has special powers.

3. A girl operates from the modern dating paradigm and doesn't know how to wisely manage sexual energy. A girl looks to a man to show her a good time, and allows men into the sacred space of her body or her home too quickly. When a relationship doesn't work out, she puts the blame on the man, and avoids self-reflection and self-evaluation for fear of what she might find if she looks closely. She wears masks and is insecure. She has a hard time holding still and is an over-doer. Sacred self-care as a consciousness and lifestyle is absent in her life, and her spirit is depleted. She doesn't listen well and she over-talks others. She delays and defers living full out in her life until she meets The One.

4. A woman knows how to invoke courtship and keep energy units balanced. She knows how to be a great date. She is mindful and very selective about men gaining entry into her body or her home. When a relationship doesn't work out, she stops to reflect on what worked and what didn't, and takes ownership for her part in the dynamics of the relationship. She strives to be authentic and to tell the truth to herself about herself without fear or denial. Sacred self-care is alive and well in her mind, body, and spirit. She lives and loves from a place of fullness. She is strong and secure in her femininity and is able to relax, flow, and graciously receive. She listens well. She is living full out in her life, and welcomes a man who wants to join her in doing so.

5. A girl treats a man as an object or commodity and asks shallow, predictable questions. She is quick to perceive men as fixed, static, and unchangeable. She doesn't realize that, as the natural leader, she both attracts and activates men. She has emotional baggage that she hasn't stopped to address or heal.

6. A woman treats a man as a unique being and asks questions based in authentic curiosity and fascination. She is not judging and assessing, screening, and rejecting each man through the filter of "husband candidate," but appreciates the time spent, whether she feels attraction for the guy or not. She realizes that she is the natural leader and the leader naturally,

and she is mindful of living from a place of feminine leadership. She knows that she both attracts and activates men and is mindful of raising the vibration of her own qualities and energy so that she can continue to attract and activate high-vibration qualities. She has engaged in the forgiveness process and returns to it to keep herself cleared of emotional baggage.

Now, you have the opportunity to complete a personal assessment that helps you recognize where you are on the girl-woman continuum. Though the Love Lies apply to both single and married women, there is an addendum to the assessment for married women that is relative to the dynamics specific to marriage, though we're not covering the Marriage Love Lies in this book. There are 10 additional items in the For-Married-Women-Only addendum to the assessment.

So if you're currently married, I invite you to fill out these additional assessment items. If you are divorced, I recommend that you reflect on your previous marriage(s), and go ahead and also complete the assessment portion for married women. Read through each of the characteristics and put a checkmark in the left or right column that reflects where you currently are.

As I continued to do my divine self-work, sacred self-care, and forgiveness work, I began to migrate from the behaviors and ways of being in the left column of this assessment to the behaviors and ways of being in the right column. When I first completed this assessment, much to my surprise, I earned an A in being in my girl. I was an enlightened woman, or so I thought. I was a personal empowerment specialist and a two-time national best-selling author. In my haughtiness I thought, maybe someone *else* scores high in the "girl" column, but not me! The truth of the matter was that, in the domain of my marriage love relationship, I was more in my girl than in my woman. I had to eat some humble pie.

After going through each item, tally up your totals. How many checkmarks are in the girl column? How many checkmarks are in the woman column? Also tally the additional items for married women, if that applies to you.

You'll notice that there is no legend or grading scale at the end of this assessment. This is not about judging yourself as having done good or bad. It's about being much more aware of how your ways of believing, thinking, behaving, relating, and communicating have been showing up and manifesting in your relationships. It's about becoming aware of behaviors you've been exhibiting or patterns of thinking and interacting that are aligned more with being in your girl or being in your woman. The objective is for your check-marks to continue to migrate to the right, to the woman column.

For graduates of Love Academy who choose to come back and review the course (we call this auditing the course), the pattern is clear. They mark more and more items in their woman column each time they audit. It can be power-ful to return to this assessment every 90 days to track your progress.

Exercise 14.1
Making the Shift from Girl to Woman Self-Assessment

Note: You will need to be ruthlessly honest with yourself in completing this assessment. In order to check a box in the right column, all of the statement must be true for you.

Behaviors, Thoughts, Emotions, and Ways of Being When I'm "In My Girl"	Behaviors, Thoughts, Emotions, and Ways of Being When I'm "In My Woman"
❏ I constantly entertain romantic fanta-sies in my head that remain there instead of being able to manifest them in my life.	❏ I know how to convert the wishes and desires in my head into reality in my relationship(s).
❏ I treat love like a thing to be acquired. I am "looking for" or "trying to find" Mr. Right or The One. I believe there's only one, singular designated man out there with whom I can have a soul-level connection.	❏ I recognize that there are multiple possibilities of soul mates that may exist. I know that the possibility of achieving a soul-level connection does not reside with a sole, designated man.
❏ I date to find a man that is a husband candidate or marriage material. I con-stantly judge and assess men.	❏ I understand that courtship is a pro-cess that requires managing the pace and tone, keeping energy units (EUs) balanced, and wisely managing sexual energy. I know how to be a great date and I know what inspires a man to want to be in my presence again.
❏ I have a Requirements List and I'm constantly scorecarding men.	❏ I have a list of qualities, not features, that I actually embody and thus can attract. I consistently activate positive high-vibration qualities and responses in men.
❏ I perceive myself as incomplete or lacking, and thus I'm looking for the man who can meet my needs.	❏ Self-care is clear in my beliefs, behav-iors, and practices. I am clear about what I share/bring/contribute to a relationship.

❏ I lack a consistent daily practice of sacred self-care and intentional connection time with myself and with God (or what I choose to name the Universal Source/Higher Power in my life).	❏ I have a *consistent daily practice* of sacred self-care and intentional connection time with myself and with God. Both are very present in my daily life.
❏ I frequently experience a feeling of needing to hold on to a man. I see a relationship as a security blanket.	❏ I come from the understanding that I am a living gift and others engage with me accordingly.
❏ I have experienced infatuation, lust, manipulation, sex ad-DICK-tion, co-dependence, a lust relationship, or sexual attraction but not a love relationship.	❏ I have experienced or am in a mature love relationship (and I am actively growing and developing myself spiritually, mentally, emotionally, and "communicationally").
❏ I have a hard time graciously receiving, and/or allowing myself to be helped, supported, or assisted.	❏ I am able to articulate what works for me and give clear feedback to let a man know when I am pleased.
❏ I have disappointments from internal expectations that constantly go unfulfilled. I've wanted a man to be responsible for my happiness.	❏ I am clear about what I want to experience and co-create in my relationship. I have a sustained inner experience of joy, and I take responsibility for my own happiness.
❏ I am overly self-conscious about my body. I constantly judge and compare myself, my body, and my life to other women.	❏ I am self-appreciating instead of self-conscious or self-criticizing. I treat my body like a temple.
❏ I nag, complain, and criticize in an attempt to get a man to change.	❏ I speak Manese, make requests, and know that I can effect change in a man.
❏ I regularly comment on what's wrong instead of what's right.	❏ I know how to open a man's heart. I understand the power of listening, expressed appreciation, and demonstrated respect, and it is obvious in how I engage with the men in my life.
❏ I use the silent treatment often, to pout, to punish a man, or to let him know he's made me angry.	❏ I use the silent treatment very rarely. I bring my voice forward to clearly communicate in Manese and make requests. Men in my life are clear about what I like, what works for me, and how I like to be touched.
❏ I carry emotional baggage, such as anger, guilt, shame, jealousy, regret, or resentment, from my past.	❏ I have actively healed past hurts and fears, released them, and removed their shadow from the present.

❏ My radiance is off or very dim.	❏ My radiance is on, and I know because others comment on my glow.
❏ I am constantly concerned about being hurt, or being hurt again, and I keep my heart cautiously covered or closed.	❏ I am courageous in my loving and am willing to open my heart, and keep it open, knowing that experiencing hurt is a possibility.
❏ I avoid silence and stillness time in my life, or struggle trying to find time for silence and stillness.	❏ I welcome and am engaged in quiet time and alone time. Some silence and stillness time are part of my day.
❏ I react emotionally and am easily angered. My hot buttons are active and easily triggered. I "go off," yell, cry, or scream often.	❏ I respond emotionally from a place of choice and mindfulness.
❏ I perceive sacrifice in relationships as loss, my loss. This also applies to family relationships.	❏ I experience sacrifice as a choice that brings gain.
❏ I suffer continuously from disappointment. I have a lot of "shoulds" and "expectations" projected onto men. I tend to idolize men.	❏ I allow a man to be human, without constant judgment and internal criticism.
❏ I am passive, apathetic, hardened, or resigned. I am generally the "follower" in my relationships with men.	❏ I am joyous, radiant, and an excellent receiver. I understand that I am the natural leader and the leader naturally in my relationships, and I know how to embody feminine leadership.
❏ I associate being in a relationship with losing my identity, or I see the relationship as being a savior.	❏ I recognize that a healthy love relationship is not a loss of identity but a contribution to it.
❏ I have experienced dating but not being courted. I haven't learned how to manage the sexual attraction energy yet. When dating, sex enters usually by the third date. Sex is either the glue, a drug, a crutch, or "the carrot" in my relationships.	❏ I know how to set the pace and tone of the relationship by invoking courtship. I take my time and wisely manage the sexual energy.
❏ I try to fill the void within that results from a lack of self-love with substitutes, distractions, or external "fillers" (these can include food, social media, TV, and shopping).	❏ I invest time and energy in feeding and filling my spirit. I am familiar with what this means. My spirit is fed and full.

❏ I speak only Womanese. I am unilingual.	❏ I speak Womanese and Manese. I am bilingual.
Total checkmarks of these 26 in the girl column: _____	Total checkmarks of these 26 in the woman column: _____

Exercise 14.2
Self-Assessment Addendum for Married Women

These 10 additional items should be considered, in addition to the ones you marked in exercise 14.1.

Behaviors, Thoughts, Emotions, and Ways of Being When I'm "In My Girl" in my marriage	Behaviors, Thoughts, Emotions, and Ways of Being When I'm "In My Woman" in my marriage
❏ Feels like I'm doing and giving a lot more than my husband.	❏ There is a felt and seen balance of power and energy in my marriage.
❏ I feel that my husband doesn't listen well and that he frequently "zones me out."	❏ I speak Manese to my husband, and I get my desired responses or actions from my husband.
❏ I don't know how to bring about different or better behavior in my husband without nagging, complaining, or getting irritated if he doesn't do things the way I think he should.	❏ I know how to "season" my husband and the fruit of my positive influence shows.
❏ I often feel disappointed or frustrated.	❏ I am deeply satisfied and fulfilled.
❏ I didn't consciously prepare or equip myself for covenant marriage, mentally, emotionally, spiritually, or by upgrading my communication skills.	❏ I prepared and equipped myself prior to marriage. I fortified my primary relationship with myself first, and then intentionally developed myself emotionally, mentally, spiritually, and "communicationally."
❏ I feel stuck or trapped, and often speak or even act like a victim. I don't feel I'm "getting my needs met."	❏ I recognize that my husband is the head and I am the lead, and we enjoy the healthy interplay of these two complementary functions, without power struggles.
❏ I suffer in silence, leave a lot unsaid, and may even have resentment toward my husband.	❏ I bring my voice forward in my marriage. I have actively healed and released my past hurts, resentments, and fears, and do not have them overshadowing or haunting me in the present.

❏ I stay married out of convenience, "for the kids," for fear of being alone, for financial reasons, or out of complacency.	❏ I understand that my partner is an added bonus to the joy and fulfillment that should already be in my life. He complements, not completes, me. I regularly experience excitement and a feeling of newness in our relationship, instead of boredom, complacency, or living like roommates.
❏ I am plagued with unmet expectations and disappointments; I have a lot of ought-to's, should's, and supposed-to's projected onto my husband, whom I perceive as often falling short in my eyes.	❏ I gladly let my husband know instead of assuming, inferring, or dropping hints. I lovingly share with him, in Manese, what I think "he should already know." I use clear requests where necessary.
❏ I am often too tired for sex, or disinterested. Sex has become too infrequent, mechanical, or withheld, or is not enjoyable for me.	❏ Sex is occurring. It is deeply enjoyable and satisfying.
Total checkmarks of these 10: _____	Total checkmarks of these 10: _____
GRAND TOTAL out of 36: _____	GRAND TOTAL out of 36: _____

Exercise 14.3
Make the Shift, Step by Step

First, recognize that a distinction does, in fact, exist between being in your girl versus being in your woman. You can't plead ignorant now.

Second, become aware of the differences in believing, thinking, and behaving.

Third, review the items you marked in your girl column and circle or mark the top three you want to focus on first. Select no more than three to work on at a time.

Fourth, make the conscious decision to respond from your woman instead of react from your girl.

Fifth, begin to "catch yourself" exhibiting girl thoughts or behaviors, and correct your course. To correct your course, take a slow, deep breath, calm down, refocus, and stay present so that you can consciously respond rather than falling back on old knee-jerk emotional reactions.

Sixth, be patient and gentle with yourself. You may slip back into old girl patterns from time to time. It's okay. It happens. Notice it, take a deep breath, get up, dust yourself off, and continue forward with your chin up.

As we move through the B.L.I.S.S.S. process, you'll be given more insights and exercises to support you in continuing to make the shift from girl to woman in your love relationships.

Chapter Fifteen

L = Let Go of Old Beliefs

Thus far, we've seen and experienced how the
Love Lies can ensnare us, hold us hostage,
warp our perceptions, shape our behaviors,
and even determine our emotional reactions.

Have you heard the adage, "You bring about what you think about"? Your thoughts, which arise out of your beliefs, are a creative force and have drawing/magnetizing power. Indeed, your dominant thoughts in life, and your dominant thoughts about men and relationships will always win out—even if they are damaging or unhealthy. Our beliefs are so powerful because they operate much like software does in a computer—determining what it can and cannot do and what it does and doesn't do. Our beliefs are the equivalent of our human "thoughtware." Our beliefs are what we've come to accept as true though they can be based on delusions and illusions. They are usually inherited mental constructs that are based on others' beliefs, and/or old programming. Your life is a reflection of your beliefs, and the same applies to your beliefs about relationships and men.

I've found that beliefs, once acknowledged and recognized, can be traded in for new beliefs that are more empowering and more aligned with what gives us an experience of deep satisfaction and fulfillment. It's critical to your detox process to uncover and unearth your beliefs, and examine and even challenge what you've accepted as true, so that you can consciously choose to release the "old" and embrace new beliefs that are more empowering and in line with what you say you want to manifest and experience.

Extricating yourself from the snare of the Love Lies requires that you cut the cords of old beliefs and release yourself from disabling beliefs that are holding you captive in unhealthy patterns, stinkin' thinkin', or self-negating behaviors. Getting in touch with these beliefs, acknowledging them instead of being oblivious to them, consciously choosing new, more empowering beliefs, and then beginning to think, act, and live according to your new beliefs is what BeliefWork is about.

Ninety percent of the following BeliefWork process is about acknowledging and becoming aware of beliefs that previously were invisible to you, but real and apparent in their effect and impact.

The following BeliefWork exercise is adapted from the 90-Day Radiance Plan Program, a step-by-step 90-day plan I co-developed to increase your radiance. The Radiance Plan is a self-study course that was created to provide a guided process and structured plan to "up" the wattage on your feminine glow and light. If you want to know how to actively and purposefully increase your radiance, you can invest in this program at DidYouBuyTheLoveLies.com.

Exercise 15.1
BeliefWork

You'll be working with a set of the same four beliefs throughout this entire exercise. For each step of the BeliefWork exercise, I'm going to share actual responses from Mariana, a Love Academy and Radiance Plan participant, to help make the process more concrete for you.

Step 1: Notice and describe behaviors
Stop and reflect on the behaviors you have or exhibit with men, especially those that are negative or undesirable. List the behaviors that you notice. Start each sentence with "I notice…"

Examples of "I notice" statements:

I notice that I have sex very early in the relationship with a man when I really like him.
I notice that I end up being the chaser or pursuer most of the time.
I notice that I tend to meet men online more than in person.
I notice that my interactions with men often don't last beyond a second date.

For step 1, Mariana wrote:

1a.   I notice that I cling to men.

1b. I notice that I create a romance in my head that has very little to do with reality, and I sometimes use men to hide from the world.

1c. I notice that I use men as trophies to make the world deem me worthy of respect, admiration, and love. How my date looks is very important to me because of the image I feel I need to portray.

1d. I notice that I am having sex way too early with men, and before any real quality connection is established.

Now it's your turn to notice and acknowledge your behaviors with men. If you want to write down more than four, you certainly may. This is just to get you started so that you can become familiar with doing BeliefWork. Use more space if you need it.

1a. I notice that _____
1b. I notice that _____
1c. I notice that _____
1d. I notice that _____

Step 2: Uncover hidden beliefs
Review your behaviors carefully. Notice any patterns that reflect your new awareness of the Love Lies or Love Truths such as using sex as the glue, being overly accommodating, acting desperate, being demanding, or perhaps more positive patterns such as being relaxed and at ease, or noticing that you take your time and set the pace of the relationship. Do you have any "aha's?"

Now we're going to take each behavior listed above and plug it into the following new sentence structure. This process will get to your hidden "whys" and help you drill down to the beliefs that are underlying your relationship behaviors, the beliefs and thoughts I call your "thoughtware."

For step 2 Mariana wrote:

2a. I cling to men because I believe that men I want don't want me.

2b. I create a romance in my head that has very little to do with reality, and I sometimes use men to hide from the world because I believe I don't know how to sustain real love.

2c. I use men as trophies to make the world deem me worthy of respect, admiration, and love because I believe I'm not deserving of real love and real passion so I move too quickly to making a sexual connection.

2d. I am having sex way too early with men, and before any real quality connection is established because I believe that men don't care to get to know the real Mariana. I believe men aren't capable of giving what me I need on a long-term basis.

Now it's your turn. Take your time and really think about what accurately completes the second half of the sentence. Complete this new sentence for each of the four behaviors you identified.

2a. (Insert what you wrote in 1a.)_____
     because I believe _____
2b. (Insert what you wrote in 1b.)_____
     because I believe _____
2c. (Insert what you wrote in 1c.) _____
     because I believe _____
2d. (Insert what you wrote in 1d.) _____
     because I believe _____

Step 3: Acknowledging the results

Now you're going to take the statement that follows "because I believe" and use it for your next step. In this step, you're acknowledging the resulting behaviors associated with each particular belief. Complete this new sentence for each of the four behaviors you identified.

For step 3 Mariana wrote:

3a. I believe men I want don't want me.
     This has resulted in desperate behavior with men; being way too preoccupied with thinking about each new guy I meet that I really like; giving my power away or giving up my power; and chasing and pursuing men even when they weren't attracted to me.

3b. I believe I don't know how to sustain real love.
     This has resulted in low self-esteem; losing myself; being guarded and

hesitant since I believed that men lie/cheat/abuse; being passive/aggressive with men; having scarcity beliefs—not enough joy/love/men/money to go around; constantly fearing rejection; and withholding affection or being stand-offish.

3c. I believe I'm not deserving of real love and real passion so I move too quickly to making a sexual connection.

This has resulted in trying to fill my yearning for deep emotional connection through sex; using sex to fill empty spaces in me; having sex too soon and with too many men; and using sex to keep him in the picture.

3d. I believe men don't care to get to know the real Mariana.

This results in me fighting to get what I need from this world, especially "fighting" for love; and feeling I must protect myself with a pre-emptive strike before a man hurts me.

You will now use what you inserted in the second part of the statements. You will then follow it up with a statement that describes the results of this behavior.

3a. I believe (insert what you wrote in the blank after the word "believe" in your 2a. statement) _____
This has resulted in (what behaviors?) _____

3b. I believe (insert what you wrote in the blank after the word "believe" in your 2b. statement) _____
_____
This has resulted in (what behaviors?) _____

3c. I believe (insert that you wrote in the blank after the word "believe" in your 2c. statement) _____
This has resulted in (what behaviors?) _____

3d. I believe (insert what you wrote in the blank after the word "believe" in your 2d. statement) _____
This has resulted in (what behaviors?) _____

Step 4: State your new truth as an affirmation

This step in the exercise takes your previously held beliefs and helps you replace them with a new truth, stated in the present tense as an affirmation. Affirmations, over time, start "installing" new truths into your thinking and literally "making them firm" in your mind. Mariana created affirmations that addressed her most disempowering beliefs, replacing them with more positive, powerful beliefs.

For step 4 Mariana wrote:

There is plenty of love/men/money/joy to go around, and plenty for me. Love moves toward me with ease. It is abundant. I receive love from others and from men with ease. I wisely and confidently manage the attention given my curvy body. My heart is open to giving and receiving love.

Mariana typed up this affirmation and taped it to her bathroom mirror. Each morning as she's getting ready for her day, she reads it. Recently she let me know that, as a result of uncovering her old beliefs and replacing them with new beliefs that are aligned with the Love Truths, she is relating to men in a more confident and relaxed manner, and, in turn they are responding with the respectful, consistent treatment she always desired.

This four-step BeliefWork process is all about helping you get in touch with the limiting, disempowering beliefs you've been operating from and trans- forming them into empowering beliefs. If you have trouble getting to the root of the beliefs driving your behavior, try answering these additional questions:

What do the patterns reveal that I believe about myself?

_____

What do my patterns reveal that I'm believing about men?

_____

What do my patterns reveal that I'm believing about relationships?

_____

Chapter Sixteen

I = **Invoke** Your Feminine Leadership

*In Chapter Twelve I introduced you to feminine
leadership, shared some analogies and metaphors to
help you grasp the concept, and also described feminine
leadership in demonstration and practice in our lives.*

The gifts of feminine leadership include (but are not limited to) leading from a place of compassion, listening well, gracefulness, vision and foresight, clarity, being responsive, being present, patience, flexibility, using loving touch strategically, directing or redirecting energy, trusting your intuition and inner wisdom, being able to graciously receive, collaboration, integrity, sensitivity to right timing, and using your gift of voice inflection and loving touch wisely.

We are now going to explore ways you can invoke feminine leadership in your relationships. To invoke, in this context, means to summon or bring forth your qualities of feminine leadership. Using the term "invoke" suggests that there are a multitude of inherent qualities that reside within you and just need to be awakened. This is exactly the case. For most of us, our feminine leadership muscles are weak and underdeveloped. The great news is that whether you are single or married, feminine leadership can be cultivated and developed over time, with practice.

How do you awaken your own feminine leadership? What supports actively developing and cultivating feminine leadership? The answer: sacred self-care.

I've come to recognize that a solid foundation of sacred self-care must be in place in a woman's life in order for her to experience joy, inner peace, and fulfillment; build trust in herself; value herself and her gifts; and stimulate and awaken her feminine leadership qualities.

Sacred Self-Care

Sacred means "important and highly valued," and care means "to exhibit concern for keeping something or someone safe, healthy, and in good condition." Sacred self-care is a concept I coined back in the late 1990s with the release of my first national book, *Sacred Pampering Principles*, to describe a way of relating to oneself that is grounded in being a responsible caretaker and wise guardian of one's own body and being, first, and valuing and honoring what nourishes, fortifies, and renews one's own mind, body, spirit, and energy before attempting to take care of others and give to or do for others.

As sacred self-care becomes more real in your life and you increasingly become a self-caring women, your natural feminine leadership qualities present and assert themselves naturally and readily. When you are living from a self-caring mindset, you have a consciousness that is compatible with valuing your feminine gifts, which frees them to be more present and active in your relationships.

Sacred self-care is a natural invoker of your natural feminine leadership gifts because it grows and strengthens these certain abilities as follows:

To know—recognizing, knowing, and embracing that you are the gift

To own—appreciating, "owning," and deeply valuing your feminine perspective, uniquely feminine qualities, and ways of perceiving

To be clear—taking time to sit down, sit still, and get clear in order to make wise decisions, choose the best courses of action for the expression of your feminine leadership, get clear on what qualities to call on, and the best time to bring them forth

To trust—trusting your intuition and inner wisdom, and heeding it

To discern—being highly perceptive and sensitive to details and nuances, and paying close attention to the feedback your sixth sense, your "gut," gives you (it is highly attuned to energy)

To love yourself—no matter what, and constantly be self-affirming and self-honoring in thought, word, and deed

To be courageous—courage is rooted in the Latin word *cor*, which means heart; being bold-hearted and gutsy

To be truthful—with yourself and others, and making powerful requests when necessary

To be strategic—assessing a situation or scenario and consciously determining when it's best to listen and when to bring your voice forward, and

when to act obviously or subtly, and getting your cues and clues from
the environment, interaction, or circumstances

To be relaxed—exhale tension and be at ease, while at the same time being
highly aware and awake

The process of becoming more self-caring is a path to greater and/or
deeper self-love and healthy self-worth, and is reflected in behaviors consistent with authentic self-confidence and self-value. A self-caring woman
is committed to living from a place of self-fullness, not selfishness, and
wisely manages her energy, not just her time. Three critical dimensions of
sacred self-care are having a *clear* mind, a *well* body, and a *full* spirit. A clear
mind is free of incessant inner chatter, self-deprecating inner talk, distractions, and stinkin' thinkin'; a well body is flexible, medication-free, ener-
gized, illness-free, and pain-free; and a full spirit is one that is rejuvenated
and refilled on a daily basis.

Over the years, I've continued to hear justifications from women for our
lack of self-care, lack of rejuvenation and renewal time, and for not taking
better care of our own minds, bodies, and spirits. Justifications have included:
I don't have the time; it's selfish; others will have to go without and won't get
what they need; I feel that I have to be in perpetual motion; if I do something
for myself I feel guilty; I must put others' needs before my own—that's what a
good mother/wife/grandmother does.

In this country we are notorious for chasing the almighty dollar, for pursuing happiness, and for searching for love and joy outside of ourselves. Love,
however, like joy, is not a thing to obtain. Joy is not an emotion but a state of
being that sacred self-care helps you rediscover and connect to. Joy is your
natural state. Being in a state of joy is not dependent upon external people
or circumstances. When you are *in joy*, you are experiencing an internal flow
of positive energy moving within you and through you, despite your external
circumstances, and despite what others are or are not doing.

So why does self-care and living from a sacred self-care mindset and
consciousness tend to be such a challenge for females? Remember the "acculturation timeline" mentioned in the beginning of the book and the incessant caretaking tasks related to the mini-Mommy behavior that is encouraged
once a little girl receives her baby doll? We've confused patterns of doing, non-
stop motion, and overdoing with being "givers." I've noticed that much of
what we call giving is actually a lot of doing. Overdoing has a very different

impact on the spirit and the emotions than does giving. Overdoing depletes you, and over time, overdoing has you feeling underappreciated, unappreciated, or taken for granted. Overdoing can be accompanied by feelings of guilt or obligation, and eventually resentment, in contrast to giving, which arises from a place of fullness, sharing, and overflow from within. Giving is the place we come from when we are healed and whole, and when our spiritual tanks are "full." Giving energizes you instead of depletes you, and the satisfaction is in the giving itself, not in expecting anything in return, including a thank you (though it sure is a nice bonus).

Allow me to share another sentiment from the pages of Eugenia Price's book *Woman to Woman*, the book I found in the used bookstore at the airport, since it directly reinforces the case for sacred self-care. Price reveals what she calls the big mistake, and explains, "I am aware of the secret place at the center of my being that no human being can fill. And which I have no right to try to force a mere human being to fill. . . . This is our big mistake. . . . Wives [try to force] their husbands." She illumines, "God has reserved a place for Himself only, deep in the very center of our beings. And our trouble springs from the fact that we try to fill this place with other things and other people. Nothing else really fits."

Author Joan Gattuso concurs, when she reminds us, "Remember, we cannot be happy in a relationship when we are attempting to force someone else to fill needs that only we can fill, to heal wounds that only we can heal." Ladies, we've attempted to fill this space with many substitutes that include cell phones, social media or TV addictions, food, shopping, gossip, and alcohol, to name a few.

I believe that this "big mistake" is what is also at the root of what propels and fuels the incessant seeking, striving, and pursuing in our relationships in this culture—wanting our boyfriends, partners, and/or husbands to fill the place within us that it is not their job to fill. This is why an essential part of sacred self-care is prayer and meditation, and stillness and silent time, so that we can connect to the center of our beings, this inner place of the indwelling God.

Miriam's Story

Sacred self-care was part of the foundation for Miriam, graduate of Love Academy 101 and my *For Married Women Only* tele-course (course details on the website), age 39, and married for 12 years. She had been going through cycles of frustration in her marriage.

Before these courses, I was looking to my husband to fill me up. I now realize, that's up to me. I was trying to love him from a place of being depleted, overdoing it, and having a hard time receiving from him. I'm now committed to filling my inner spiritual tank and having a more self-caring lifestyle.

Part of her self-care was creating an affirmation for herself based upon Love Truth #2 that has now become her mantra. It simply is: *I am the gift.* Before Love Academy, she felt that she should revolve around her husband, like a planet orbiting the sun. She tried to do this, though begrudgingly, and it caused irritation and frustration to bubble to the surface in the form of her being "sharp-tongued" with him. When she is in the midst of an argument, a frustrating situation, or a conflict with her husband, she now repeats her I-am-the-gift mantra within (or even whispers it quietly under her breath). It helps her stay calm and re-centers her. She explains that it helps her stay present and in her woman, instead of kicking into old behaviors of getting defensive, closing down, getting "tight-lipped," or giving him the silent treatment.

Now I am committed to loving him out of my overflow, not from a place of need and lack. I am taking responsibility for doing my part in creating a new and wonderful experience in my marriage. I've noticed that my husband and I now have fewer arguments, he's being less abrasive and more loving with me. I can feel my heart re-opening to him, I'm learning to relax, breathe, and be a better receiver. I'm conscious about speaking appreciation into him (more on this later), and he says that I'm being a better listener."

Exercise 16.1
Sacred Self-Care "Neglect" Quiz

Take this quiz to find out if you've been neglecting sacred self-care. It will help you learn how real sacred self-care is in your life right now. Check the items that partially or fully apply to you.

❑ Feel unfocused
❑ Feel unfulfilled
❑ Get angry or "pissed off" easily
❑ Frequently feel upset
❑ Feel overwhelmed
❑ Very judgmental and critical (of yourself and/or of others)
❑ Constantly restless and rushing

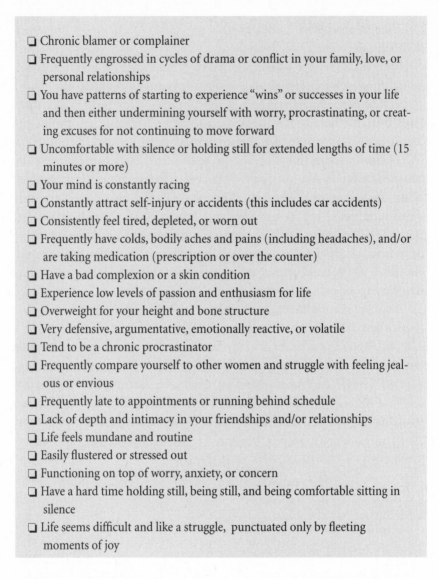

❏ Chronic blamer or complainer
❏ Frequently engrossed in cycles of drama or conflict in your family, love, or personal relationships
❏ You have patterns of starting to experience "wins" or successes in your life and then either undermining yourself with worry, procrastinating, or creating excuses for not continuing to move forward
❏ Uncomfortable with silence or holding still for extended lengths of time (15 minutes or more)
❏ Your mind is constantly racing
❏ Constantly attract self-injury or accidents (this includes car accidents)
❏ Consistently feel tired, depleted, or worn out
❏ Frequently have colds, bodily aches and pains (including headaches), and/or are taking medication (prescription or over the counter)
❏ Have a bad complexion or a skin condition
❏ Experience low levels of passion and enthusiasm for life
❏ Overweight for your height and bone structure
❏ Very defensive, argumentative, emotionally reactive, or volatile
❏ Tend to be a chronic procrastinator
❏ Frequently compare yourself to other women and struggle with feeling jealous or envious
❏ Frequently late to appointments or running behind schedule
❏ Lack of depth and intimacy in your friendships and/or relationships
❏ Life feels mundane and routine
❏ Easily flustered or stressed out
❏ Functioning on top of worry, anxiety, or concern
❏ Have a hard time holding still, being still, and being comfortable sitting in silence
❏ Life seems difficult and like a struggle, punctuated only by fleeting moments of joy

Your Quiz Analysis: There are a total of 28 items on this quiz. If you marked 10 or more items on this quiz, then self-neglect instead of sacred self-care is too dominant in your consciousness, mindset, behavior, and lifestyle. If you haven't already read it, I would strongly suggest my first best-selling book, *Sacred Pampering Principles*, as a guide to helping you make the shift from self-neglect to self-care. You can order a copy through DidYouBuyTheLoveLies.com.

Starting your day in a self-caring way

To experience a brand-new day is a gift, and it deserves your best. Never again will you have the opportunity (or privilege) of waking up into this particular day. Instead of being on auto-pilot mode, like most females, and jumping out of bed, jumping in the shower, rushing to get dressed, and then dashing out of the house, try this self-caring scenario on for size. Be committed to beginning your day so that you intentionally set the tone and the "keynote" for your day.

Start your day with what feeds your spirit and helps you feel grounded, centered, and refueled. Is it stretching, prayer, and meditation (which I recommend as a foundation for every self-caring woman); listening to uplifting, relaxing, or inspirational music; writing in your journal (please get a journal just for your morning devotion time, if you don't already have one); reading affirmations, reciting affirmations out loud, or reading from the Holy Bible or other holy books that inspire and energize you? In general, our spirits appreciate stillness, silence, nature, high-vibration thoughts, emotions, and experiences. It's important, however, to know what nourishment your spirit appreciates in particular.

The presence of "re" in your life

If your self-care mindset is in place and you are practicing it and living it, it "ups" the presence of "re" in your life. Re is a powerful verb prefix that, when combined with certain verbs, indicates the types of outcomes that are consistent with self-care. Re words, when applied to and in your life, support you in staying on course with sacred self-care. Re words such as renew, restore, and rejuvenate, tend to align with self-care while "de" words, such as depleted, depressed, detached, and dependent, tend to describe our state of mind, body, and spirit when self-care is missing or lacking.

The more positive re words of this kind that your choices, behaviors, and lifestyle reflect, the more your life will tend to be a reflection (there's a re word!) of a life that nourishes, fortifies, and renews your mind, body, and spirit.

Exercise 16.2
The "Re" Game Exercise

Now it's your turn to come up with re words. Give yourself 60 seconds to brainstorm as many positive re words as you can. If you're up for a little friendly "Re

Game," compete with a second person, or a group of three or more. The object is to see how many re words both or all of you come up with and write down in 60 seconds. You'll need a piece of paper and pen for this exercise/game.

You *can't* use the four I already gave you (wink): renew, restore, rejuvenate, and reflect.

Okay, so are you ready? Get set . . . go!

How'd you do? If you chose to do this as a group game, after the 60 seconds, each person counts up her re words. You get 1 point for each word on your list. Then have each person read her list out loud. If any of the words on anyone else's list also appears on yours, cross that re word off your list. What should be remaining on each list after everyone has had a turn are *only* the re words that are unique, and thus no one else has them on their list. Each person gets 5 points for each unique word. Tally up your totals. The person with the most points wins!

Sacred self-care is about making these re words real (another re word) and actualized in your life.

Wisely managing your energy

In a sacred self-caring lifestyle, you might be surprised to know that wisely managing your energy is paramount, and management of your time is secondary. In this culture, we're very time-focused and actually quite time-obsessed. We speak of saving time, finding time, wasting time, and time flying, when actually, we each have the same 24 hours in a day. If you find a 25th hour, or there are "saved" hours in a time bank account somewhere I don't know about, please let me know.

Sacred self-care requires that you think differently about *how, where, with whom,* and *on what* you utilize and invest your energy. For most of us this means learning to say no or no thank you more often, and without guilt. When your attention is on wisely managing your energy, you ask yourself different questions than when you are only time-focused. Here are some contemplation questions to consider when thinking through how, where, with whom, and on what to expend or invest your energy.

How and where am I currently utilizing my energy?

Are my investments of energy *aligned* with what I say is important and matters most to me?

What impact will saying yes have on my energy?

What impact will saying no have on my energy?

Am I entering into a situation that has a balanced give and receive of energy?

Am I saying yes to something that will feel "heavy," burden me, or feel like an obligation?

Appreciating the Male Gifts

An important context for understanding your natural gifts of feminine leadership is in relation to the unique gifts of men. In the domain of relationships, men are uncomplicated, in general. I consider them to be "beautifully uncomplicated." When you understand the male gifts, it helps you understand, even more fully, why the feminine leadership gifts are so important, and how to cultivate them and bring them forth unapologetically.

I am going to distill the male gifts down to what I consider to be these core seven:

1. *Literal:* What you see is usually what you get; they say what they mean.
2. *Actional:* They think and act in "verb" terms (action words).
3. *Feat-oriented:* They work well with specific, clear, well-defined tasks. Think in terms of items on a checklist. Short, direct, clear. They enjoy accomplishing feats. Gone are the days when a man may rescue a "damsel in distress," or slay a dragon, not to mention even helping her change a tire. Nonetheless, the male "wiring" with a bias toward accomplishing feats still exists. Today, in this age of high-tech and mass computerization, the feat may be scaled down to something as simple as getting the oil in your car changed, moving or lifting something heavy for you, fixing or repairing something, or putting your carry-on luggage in the airplane's overhead bin for you.
4. *Solution-oriented:* Men's minds think in terms of solutions, fixing the problem, making things work, or making it better. Remember this when you vent to a man who cares about you—his mind is going to move into solution-mode, though all you may want him to do, at the moment, is listen. Don't condemn him for this. Just tell him, in advance, that you only need him to listen. And he will.
5. *Single-minded focus:* Men have the gift of being able to focus well on one thing at a time.

6. *Uncomplicated:* Men are rather basic and simple.
7. *Highly "season-able":* Though we'll get into this one in more detail in Chapter Eighteen, let it suffice for now to say that men respond very well to "good seasoning."

Of course, these gifts do not apply to every male without exception. They are tendencies of most men. When you understand what the male gifts are, you are able to even more clearly discern and recognize how feminine leadership qualities are synergistic and complementary. For example, can you see how understanding the process and not just the solution or the result is complementary? Can you see how being able to hold multiple points of focus at once instead of a single point of focus is complementary? As you grow in the expression of your feminine leadership qualities, it becomes increasingly apparent how important the presence of both sets of gifts are to a male/female love relationship being harmonious and in balance.

Exercise 16.3
Valuing Your Feminine Leadership Gifts

As you reflect over the forms of the feminine leadership gifts in this chapter, and the seven male gifts just listed, in what other ways are feminine gifts a complement to male gifts? _____

_____

With this said, let's look more closely at the dynamics of feminine leadership within covenant marriage. Then we'll explore ways to bring your gift of feminine leadership forward more fully in your relationships.

The Quarterback and the Head Coach Analogy

As I mentioned earlier, I suspected the notion of the wife being the natural leader in a covenant marriage might cause some ruffled feathers because (1) it challenges a widely held interpretation about male headship in marriage, and (2) it introduces the new distinction of female leadership as a noncompeting, complementary, divine assignment within covenant marriage.

One morning, when I was putting the finishing touches on the proposal for this book to submit to my literary agent, I was having my last round of "talks" with God about my desire to leave the "woman is the natural leader and the leader naturally" Love Truth *out* of this book. This particular morning, I was making what turned out to be my last plea to delete this Love Truth.

It was January and the Super Bowl was around the corner, so it shouldn't have surprised me when, during my dialogue with God, He chose to use a football analogy to illustrate the healthy dynamics of headship and leadership in covenant marriage. God asked, *So who's the head of the football team?* "The head coach," I replied. *Yes, correct. And so who's the leader of the football team?* "The quarterback." *Yes, that's correct.*

What follows are seven important aspects of relating and engaging that God pointed out to me to support a better understanding of the dance of leadership and headship, as demonstrated by the functions and interactions of the quarterback and the head coach. From this analogy, I grasped a clearer understanding of how the headship and leadership functions engage to achieve a powerful, balanced, and harmonious devine partnership.

Even if you're only vaguely familiar with football, you should be able to relate to this analogy. And more important, it should make very clear how the nuances and dynamics of headship and leadership are intended to work and flow together in the covenant marriage.

1. The quarterback and the head coach have two very different skill sets, functions, and perspectives that work in cooperation with one another. The point of view of the quarterback, who is on the field in the midst of the action, is different from that of the head coach, who is on the sidelines. They are literally and metaphorically "standing in two different places," enabling the two to see the full picture—together.

2. The quarterback and head coach are in constant communication. Either can call a time-out. They huddle often and discuss the best strategic moves and plays for the team. They have a common, unifying goal—a victory for the team—that is the centerpiece of all of their discussions.

3. The head coach is also in constant communication with the team's defensive and offensive coordinators, who are giving him feedback, moment by moment, so that he can decide upon the best and most strategic plays to pass on to the quarterback, and to achieve the best outcomes on the field.

4. The quarterback is leading and directing the action on the field, but when the quarterback comes to the sidelines to talk to the coach, he

submits to the coach's authority when making the final decision on a play. He chooses to accept and heed the guidance and direction of the head coach because he knows that they are on the same team and both have the same objective—for the team to win the game.

5. After the quarterback and head coach agree to the play that is going to be run, once he's back on the field, the quarterback has the power and ability to choose to ignore the joint play decision and decide to "do his own thing," but that most likely wouldn't serve the team, would undermine the coach's authority, would undermine their partnership, and would also erode the head coach's trust in him. Submitting to the head coach is a choice the quarterback makes to yield to the head coach's authority. If there is no submitting, the head coach's positional authority is compromised and effectively undermined.

6. In the final minutes of the game, when every play and decision is even more critical, they huddle more frequently, especially if it's a close game. They have to be in synch, be clear, understand each other, and be in one accord about the goals and objectives they want to achieve with each movement of the ball.

7. When the game is over, whether the team wins or loses, the media interviews both the quarterback and the head coach. When there is a loss, however, the post-game reporters always ask the head coach, "What happened?" The head coach, though he can't set foot on the field during the game, is still accountable for what happens on the field and what the quarterback and the team do. He's also accountable to the owner of the team.

So which one do you think represents the dynamics of the wife's leadership in this football analogy? Yep, the quarterback. And who do you think represents the owner of the team? Yes, God.

A New Vision for Covenant Marriage

Within the covenant marriage, an important aspect of invoking your feminine leadership is being clear about how the biblical concept of submitting works in practice in the spiritual partnership. Here, we are talking about submitting working in conjunction with a certain type of authority—headship authority—that is assigned to the husband in the marriage. Just as influence, one of the forms of feminine leadership, is not to be abused or misused, the husband's headship authority is not to be abused or misused.

Just as some wives may be confused about submitting, some husbands are confused about what headship authority is in a covenant marriage relationship. A husband may interpret it as condoning domination, or sometimes even abuse; only my opinion matters; I make all of the decisions; you have to get my permission before you make a move; having standards he holds his wife to but not himself; or insisting she submit to his positional authority even though he is not yet submitted to Christ's spiritual authority in his life.

Submit is not a four-letter word

Submitting is an important aspect of feminine leadership in covenant marriage that is powerful, not weak. It requires a woman's trust in her husband's ability to function as the head, an understanding that she is submitting to God through her husband, but it also means that a wife recognizes she has the ability to usurp her husband's positional authority and wisely chooses not to because she understands that doing so can leave a husband and wife at odds or in discord instead of being united and in agreement.

So why is the word "submit" often a fighting word for most wives? Could we be operating from a misinterpretation whereby we incorrectly understand submit to mean he's "one up" and we're "one down"; that we're a "doormat"; our voices stifled; or our thoughts, input, or perspective less important? Could we likewise be operating from a misinterpretation about the husband's authority in covenant marriage whereby we misconstrue it as subjugating, dominating, or controlling?

This misinterpretation can easily occur when we confuse "positional authority" with power-based authority. Power-based authority is the power one person has *over* another to dominate, coerce, control, or bend to one's will. By design, power-based authority is incompatible with divine partnership, and is *not* the type of authority assigned to husbands in the spiritual partnership of covenant marriage. Headship is not about "head over" the wife but headship *alongside* her leadership. Remember, *dominion was given to both, together, by the Creator* (Genesis 1:26-28). When a husband and wife are walking appropriately in their spiritual assignments of headship and leadership, these two functions work hand in hand, synergistically and interdependently, by design.

The headship authority of the husband is intended to facilitate the fulfillment of a husband's function and to work in harmony with the wife's feminine leadership. Both are necessary in order to support and maintain order, balance, and fulfillment in the spiritual partnership. Furthermore, an important element of spiritual partnership unique to covenant marriage is that the husband has positional authority, *along with* accountability for both himself *and* his wife. Accountability means he has the responsibility to "answer for" the decisions, choices, and behaviors of both himself *and* his wife. In other words, the husband is held accountable for the actions of both himself and his wife.

This applies especially to significant decisions and directions that affect the partnership. This means that after sharing your perspective—applying your gifts of feminine leadership and influence—you yield to the headship of the husband and let him do his job of wise and informed decision-making in the best interest of the partnership. To submit also means growing in your ability to trust his decisions, stand as a unified front alongside him, and embrace the decision(s) he's made and embrace them as your own instead of seeing it as "his" decision. This applies even to decisions that, once in a while, may miss the mark or don't turn out.

When you practice submitting in support of a divinely guided and balanced partnership, your feminine leadership muscles are further exercised and strengthened, as is the harmony and fulfillment of your relationship.

Exercise 16.4
Stir Up Your Gifts of Feminine Leadership

This exercise applies whether or not you are currently in a relationship. Being able to bring forth feminine leadership within your relationships is essential whether you are single or married.

Below are four steps that are related to invoking and awakening your natural feminine leadership gifts. The first three steps have an accompanying journaling question. Remember, invoking your feminine leadership gifts is an ongoing process, not a one-time event.

1. Recognize and "get" your gifts of feminine leadership (see the beginning of this chapter, and also the Love Truth #10 section on page 120 if you need a refresher on these gifts).
    Journaling question: What are the gifts I have already felt or seen in myself?

    _____

    _____

    _____

    _____

2. Trust and embrace your gifts of feminine leadership and acknowledge that they have value. Check your inner self-talk for doubts or judgment.
    Journaling question: What doubts, judgment, or concerns might I have about more fully bringing these gifts forward? _____

    _____

    _____

    _____

3. Look for opportunities to use, grow, and develop even more of your feminine leadership gifts.
    Journaling question: What feminine leadership qualities do I want to bring more fully forward in my relationship? _____

    _____

    _____

    Journaling question: What "invokers" do I want to use to stir up even more of my feminine leadership qualities? _____

    _____

    _____

Continue making the shift to being in your woman. This naturally supports the emergence of your feminine leadership gifts. This includes being both gracious and patient with yourself as your leadership confidence and self-trust continues to get stronger.

Chapter Seventeen

S = **Stop** the Communication Insanity

———————————

"Communication is the key" is the mantra commonly touted when a relationship runs aground and is in trouble.

———————————

E ven with all of the marriage counselors and therapists in this country, and more than 25,000 book titles on communication in relationships, we still have serious and major challenges with communication in our relationships. Communication is a skill, and thus it is a learned ability that can be upgraded and enhanced through training and with practice.

In particular, thanks to the Love Lies, many females and males find themselves constantly experiencing what I call "the insanity cycle." The insanity cycle creates a negative, downward-spiraling cycle of verbal and nonverbal communication exchanges (and the energy and emotions behind the words) that can easily be set in motion, even with a simple but accusatory statement such as, "You're not listening!" This is probably one of the most common triggers for the insanity cycle. That's because when you accuse him of "not listening," it's usually not the case. He's hearing *every* word but comprehending little or none of it because it's in Womanese. To his ears, you're speaking a *foreign* language. Remember the teacher on the Charlie Brown cartoons? To his ears it can sound like *Whah, Whah, Whah, Whah.* Talking louder or saying it "a thousand more times" isn't going to increase his comprehension. Trust me—he is not purposefully trying to frustrate you. The *last* thing a man wants to encounter is a female's anger and too much negative emotional intensity coming at him from a female.

The insanity cycle continues to descend into a downward spiral when, after things in a relationship build to a point of frustration, the couple attempts to have "a talk" about what they think are merely communication problems. But then, as the female starts to "vent" and emote verbally, she gets worked up from the pent-up emotions. Her Womanese language and communication style runs, head on, into his Manese language and communication style. It's at this point that she starts over-talking him when it's his turn, that is, if he's able to get a word in edge-wise. Instead of a conversation occurring, which means both of them are taking turns speaking, listening, and being heard by the other, it becomes a venting session for the female, and one in which her objective seems to be to make him wrong and establish that she's right or justified in her reaction or perception. Her tone is often accusatory and blaming, and puts him on the defensive. In most cases, it's the female taking up 80 percent of the airtime, while the male remains virtually silent or is put on the defensive. He becomes more withdrawn emotionally and may literally withdraw from her presence. This hurts her and causes her more frustration, then her icy silence, and the downward spiral of the insanity cycle continues.

Any of this sound familiar?

Causes of Communication Breakdowns

As I mentioned earlier, the focus in our current relationship paradigm is often on the communication itself. But I've found that communication breakdowns are an effect and not a cause of relationship problems. So what occurs before communication breaks down or stops flowing? There are usually four general root causes (in no particular order) that result in communication breakdowns:

Root Cause #1: Most of us come into relationships emotionally and spiritually immature and underprepared.

Because the Love Lies have us viewing relationships through a lens where true self-love and self-care is lacking, inner voids are rampant, and our focus is on finding The One, they retard our emotional and spiritual development. What a difference it would make if both men and women had to take prerequisite courses on self-love; forgiveness and healing past emotional pain; being unselfish; giving, sharing, and receiving love; and learning to operate more from the heart and less from the ego, for example.

Root Cause #2: Prior to communication deteriorating, or getting sparse or choppy, something first happens to the "invisible wires" extending between a man and a woman. An upset, which comes in different forms, usually causes a snip or a kink in the "invisible wires" that figuratively stretch across the space between a male and female, thus interrupting the flow of communication. These upsets typically come in the following forms:

- A violation—perceived as a breach of boundaries. These may include a violation of emotional or sexual trust, a violation of physical space with unwanted physical contact, or a violation of one's privacy (opening the other's mail, searching through a wallet, bank account, cell phone texts, or call history, etc.).
- An offense—an act or behavior perceived as displeasing or blatantly disrespectful, such as gawking at another woman in public, him cursing at you; or having inappropriate conversations with other females on social media or via text.
- A betrayal—a feeling that someone or something was misrepresented, or feeling deluded, abandoned, tricked, or deceived.
- A disappointment—a result of feeling expectations weren't fulfilled, needs weren't met, or the form or type of wanted support wasn't provided.

Root Cause #3: A "hot button" is pushed that is the result of unhealed wounds or sensitivities from the past, whether from childhood or a past relationship. When you are in your girl and he is in his boy, neither of you have actively engaged in healing and forgiveness work, and either of you can be easily triggered in a conversation. Residue from past toxic emotions is being stirred up, you're listening through "ears" still unhealed from your past; your perceptions can be warped; and you're trying to love from a heart that may still be partially closed down because of past hurt or pain.

Root Cause #4: You both are "communicationally" immature; thus, comprehension isn't occurring and mutual understanding is not being achieved. You feel and think that you're being crystal clear. The fact is, you two are speaking different languages—Womanese and Manese. Unless you are speaking to a man in his native tongue, Manese, it's highly likely he's hearing you but not comprehending you. Most of us did not work on intentionally upgrading our communication skills before we got into a relationship, and especially marriage—and nor did we know that we should, because this certainly isn't something the Love Lies paradigm emphasizes.

Dealing with the Root Causes: The Love Lies emotionally and spiritually handicap us and it is reflected in our ability (or inability) to communicate positively and effectively. We've looked in detail at how the Love Lies can impact the ways we communicate in our relationships when we're still in our girl, but I want to spend a little time here looking at the other three root causes so you can better understand and avoid the insanity cycle.

Kinks in the invisible wires

When the invisible wires between a man and woman have been snipped, clipped, or kinked, a short circuit occurs, so to speak. A kink or snipping of some of the invisible wires occurs when one or both parties have experienced an upset, an event that usually leads to a negative emotional disturbance or agitation if not addressed, whether addressed within oneself or through conversation.

With regard to communication in relationships, the female reaction to an upset tends to be similar to that of the cervix—she closes down, even if by a few degrees. There's a contraction of her heart. When this occurs, she can go into silent mode or get sullen, despondent, or icy. The male reaction to an upset tends to be withdrawing, partially or fully, and checking out. Hence you might experience a man retreating to his "man cave"; storming out of the house to "cool off"; escaping to video games, TV, or the internet; "checking out"; or going to a bar to ingest a substance, such as alcohol, that can alter his mood or disposition. All these can be forms of male withdrawal.

If these patterns continue over time and no action is taken or effort made to restore the connection, then a female's heart can continue to close, degree by degree, and the male can continue to withdraw, "inch by inch" (no pun intended). The longer this dynamic goes avoided or unaddressed, the more difficult it can be for a couple to re-open their hearts to each other. This is also why the forgiveness work included in Chapter Nineteen is so important.

Moreover, if these upsets continue to occur, a ping-pong effect can occur in which one person triggers the other and emotional reactions start to fly back and forth. Because the couple often doesn't realize what the root cause is, they reach the deepest levels of the insanity cycle, reacting and counter-reacting as their communication progressively deteriorates.

When there is a build-up of unaddressed violations, betrayals, offenses, and disappointments, you must re-establish the "broken" circuit so that communication can flow unimpeded once again.

Getting to the heart of the upset

In many ways, hot-button triggers and residual hurt from upsets look the same in the way they affect your daily interactions—the thing you think you're mad or hurt about isn't really the thing that's bothering you. For example, you find yourself getting enraged when your husband or boyfriend asks you to let him finish watching the football game before you share about your day. But if you could pause for a moment, you might remember that your father was emotionally unavailable, physically unavailable, or withdrawn, and you always wanted more of his time and attention but didn't get it. You yearned for a deeper connection with him. Though your boyfriend or husband has made a simple, innocent statement, it triggers that old wound and your emotional system sounds the alarm—Uh oh, I'm being ignored again! I don't like feeling pushed to the side and being treated as a non-priority! The result: you find yourself having an over-reaction to the situation in the present because of unresolved issues from the past.

Because of this triggered hot-button issue, his response could be met with a comment from you stated with a strained voice or tinged with agitation. "All I want is a few minutes of your time!" you insist.

He looks at you, surprised at your strong reaction, and says, "You don't need to get so worked up. I'm just trying to watch the game."

You rebut with, "I'm not over-reacting! I'm not getting worked up!" You can feel your heart starting to shut down and close. You turn and storm off, determined to give him the silent treatment for the rest of the evening.

Think of your heart as a portal. In its open state, your heart opening is wide and round. Your mouth is also a portal, an opening. If someone were to ask you to open your mouth wide so that they could look at the back of your throat, your mouth would be wide open. If someone asked you to purse your lips like you were going to whistle, you'd tighten or contract your mouth. This is also how it works with your heart, metaphorically speaking.

In its "natural" state, your heart is wide open. When you've had certain past experiences with others, especially a parent, it can negatively affect your understanding of love, create pain or confusion about love, or cause us to question how deserving we are of love. If we haven't taken steps to intentionally unload emotional baggage from our past, and actively heal old emotional wounds, then these sore spots are still there within, like a fully loaded shot gun. When one of our hot buttons gets triggered, we react, and the shotgun starts going off, blasting anyone in its path. We can blast the other with our anger, with yelling, screaming, going silent, withdrawing, or intentionally "cutting" him with our words. In these instances, our hearts shut down, or more accurately, contract or tighten like pursed lips.

Remember, in those moments when you get triggered, you are not being present to the current conversation at hand. Emotional wounds are "leftovers" from your past. The reason the button is called a hot button and not a cold button is because it's still "charged" with negative emotional energy.

The following exercise will assist you in uncovering the roots of your hot buttons in your interactions with men, recognizing what has really "snipped" the communication wires, and thus have fewer and fewer communication breakdowns.

Exercise 17.1
What's Triggering Me?

Part 1

During a conversation, you can hold up your index finger (a way to say "give me a moment"), close your eyes, and take two deep breaths, inhaling slowly to the count of three and exhaling slowly to the count of four. This is a way to use your breath to slow down your heart rate, help you get clear, get re-centered in a few seconds, and "cool off" your hot button once it's triggered.

Part 2

Here are some questions to ask yourself (write down your answers) once an upset has occurred:

- There's what I think I'm upset about, and then there's what I'm *truly* upset about. What really caused me to tighten or close my heart?
- What were the thoughts I was having immediately before getting upset?
- If it's not really about the other person, but something going on down inside of me, what is being triggered in me? What is the source of this feeling? With whom from my past do I associate this feeling?

Once you stop, ask and answer these questions, and keep digging deeper, you should have some insights into the cause of the upset, beyond what seems most obvious. Maturity shows when you're able to stop and think for a moment about what the upset is *really* about, respond thoughtfully instead of reacting, and listen well, especially in a heated situation or interaction. Chapter Nineteen on healing and forgiveness will also aid you in releasing the emotional wounds and negative emotional energy that is "powering" your hot buttons.

We'll apply this practice along with others to smooth out the kinks later in this chapter. Now, let's look at the other root causes that may be affecting your communication and keeping you trapped in the insanity cycle.

Improving Comprehension

Before communication can work, we need to understand how our men are "hearing" us and what they are and are not understanding. On the left below are our Womanese communication tendencies and on the right is "what works" when you're speaking Manese.

Womanese Communication Tendencies	Learning to Speak Manese
To speak using concepts	To speak using words that convey observable, clear actions/words
Infer, drop hints, indirect	Be literal, direct, and specific
Narrates, commentates	State your point
Describes the details	Give the facts and pertinent information
Explains, gives the background	The bottom line, the outcome/results
Vents, talk therapy, verbal discharge of energy	Discharge the energy physically or through direct physical actions instead of talking
Comfortable expressing emotions verbally	Comfortable with direct physical expression of emotions
Unaware of the impact of your voice	Be highly aware of your voice inflection, inflection on a man's ears and keep your voice calm and sweet
We say, "How do you feel. . ."	Say, "What do you think. . ."

For a long time, a bone of contention in my marriage was my husband not checking in by phone frequently enough when he was out and about, or being very inaccurate when he communicated how long he'd be. He might say, "I'll be back in a couple of hours" and then it was three or four. He might say, "I'll be home at 1:00 a.m.," after being out with the fellas and then get home at 2:30 a.m. This was a chronic pattern with him that would frustrate me to no end. Before I knew how to speak Manese to him, I'd go on and on about how I was frustrated and irritated by his lack of communication. And during the "conversation" (or more accurately, my venting session) I'd repeatedly ask why he couldn't just place a simple call. *How hard was that to do?* My voice would be raised, and I definitely had that "I'm highly irritated with you" tone in my voice, especially after the umpteenth conversation about this. At the end of my venting, we both were highly frustrated, with him saying that I was blowing things out of proportion. Of course, this only frustrated me more.

Then I learned to speak Manese. I came to realize, after devoting several deep reflection sessions to revisiting numerous communication interactions we'd had, and playing them back slowly in my head, frame by frame, that our friction was often the result of speaking two different languages. I discovered that there was a more effective way to structure my communication when speaking to my husband.

Previously, in our conversations, I'd taken up all of the airtime, sharing my emotions, venting my frustration, or describing how a situation or incident made me feel, which caused him to tune me out.

I tried a different approach that got me much better results. First I offered a calm, clear, factual explanation of the problem as I perceived it, second I communicated its effect on my feelings, and third I explained why it didn't work for me. Then I closed my mouth and listened to him and his response without cutting him off or over-talking him. Last, I articulated a request. *Would you check-in when your plans change and let me know if you're going to be home much later than the time you designated?*

The next time it happened, I said to him, "You said you'd be back home by 1:00 a.m. and got back at 2:30 a.m. It frustrates me when this happens because I perceive this (using the word *perceive* is me taking ownership for my perception and keeps the conversation from digressing to a blame game) as being inconsiderate and disrespectful. Plus my mind starts to think something bad may have happened to you. You're taking longer than you anticipated to do something or being out much later with the fellas isn't the problem. I care about your safety, and so a simple update puts my mind at ease." I was able to clarify that my concern was about his safety and well-being, and not about distrust or trying to control him. Once I made it clear, using this new approach, that I was not trying to micromanage him nor was I attacking him, he was able to really hear me.

Let's revisit the last ingredient of my new, enlightened way of communicating with my husband—making a request. As I discussed in Chapter Ten, a request is a specific type of action-based question that facilitates the male's understanding and participation in the desired change, action, or behavior. So I asked my husband, "In the future, would you take a few seconds to call me with an update if the initial timeline you gave me changes? I'd really appreciate it." His answer was yes.

And though he was a little rusty with it at first (because he was adopting a new behavior), I worked hard not to criticize him for slipping up. I expressed appreciation each time he remembered to fulfill this request, as positive reinforcement. (Too often, ladies, we highlight when he doesn't get it right instead of providing positive reinforcement and expressing appreciation when he does.) He's now a pro at it. And even to this day, when he calls to check in, I make it a point, *every time*, to say, "Thanks for calling, honey. I really appreciate it."

Helping him listen better

As females, we literally discharge emotional energy through our mouths when we share about an upsetting situation. Talking it out for us means "talking out" the emotional energy. Venting is one of the primary ways that we release pent-up emotional energy.

However, if you share your frustrations with your husband/boyfriend/ man, you need to realize that his inclination is to want to fix it and solve the problem, or to give you advice or offer you a solution. This is why I suggest to women that, when possible, vent to a girlfriend *first*, to release most of the emotional energy from the situation, and *then* talk to your husband/boyfriend about it. Men get weary and have a hard time staying present and tuned in when we "talk their ears off."

Also, let him know, *before* you begin venting, that you only need him to listen. Let him know *in advance* of starting to emote and discharge. Then inform him that you'll let him know if you'd like him to give you some advice or tell you what he thinks you should do. This is extremely helpful to men.

Otherwise, they'll kick into what, for them, is a comfortable and "natural" aspect of how they communicate—solution mode.

Last but not least, understand that women tend to listen with their ears *and* eyes, while men tend to listen with their ears. I remember times when I'd be sharing something exciting or something of great importance to me and my husband would be sitting in his favorite chair reading the newspaper. As I was sharing, he kept perusing the paper and flipping through the pages. To me, it looked like he was not listening. I'd then ask, exasperated, "Are you even listening to what I'm saying?" He'd pause, turn to look at me, and recap every word I'd just said. I came to realize that he was listening, and hearing every word, but in his Manese style. When men communicate, they don't necessarily have or require eye-to-eye contact with each other.

But when females communicate, especially something sensitive, we have eye-to-eye contact with each other. So I came to realize that I needed him to also "listen with his eyes," when I was talking to him. It felt like he was *really* listening and being more present when he gave me eye contact. I learned to make a request: I *sweetly* said, "Honey, would you listen to me with your eyes, too, and give me eye contact while I'm talking to you?" Of course he was glad to oblige me.

Remember, it's the communication differences at play here, so don't make him wrong for operating from his male communication comfort zone.

Being Able to Say "You Were Right" or "I'm Sorry"

There have been times in my marriage when it's been appropriate for me to be able to come back to my husband and acknowledge when I've been wrong and he's been right. It is also a sign of maturity. In the early years of my marriage, I had a hard time doing this. My ego was in the way. My husband is an especially good judge of character, and on a few occasions over the years, he's forewarned me when he sensed bad vibes, bad intentions, or questionable motives from someone whose acquaintance I had just made. In those instances in which time revealed that he was right (which has been every time), it was important for me to circle back and acknowledge that he was right. This shows him I was listening, that I was paying attention to and valued what he shared with me.

In addition to being able to say, "You were right," is the ability to say, "I'm sorry."

Our husbands don't "get their feelings hurt" as readily as we tend to, or get bent out of shape about the same things we do, but they do suppress a lot of their anger instead of communicating verbally about it. They prefer to keep the peace rather than broach a subject that might put them on the receiving end of an emotional outburst. Most husbands abhor "having a talk" with their wives because they automatically expect that they will not be listened to, will be "talked over," will not get airtime, will be argued down on every point, will be told they're wrong, or will be subjected to an overly emotional reaction.

In some instances what's called for is an apology from you. You have to pay close attention to your man's body language and facial expressions (since he's not likely to verbally say anything). Especially watch his eyes; they can give you cues to let you know when something you've said has been a blow to the gut or something you've done has affected him very negatively. Think: *Did I just make an unjust accusation, jump to conclusions, or say something derogatory about his character?* His body language will let you know. At a moment like this, when a woman is able to say "I'm sorry" to her man, it earns more points in his mind and heart than you may ever know. His heart will stay open to you. It also shows him that you're mature enough and thus woman enough to admit when you're "out of pocket," and that you're in tune enough with him to notice when you say or do something that is hurtful or irritating to him—something few females are able to do.

I've also become more mindful about the right timing when I have something important to share with him—when he's watching the ESPN sports highlights, the NBA play-offs, a PGA golf tournament, or a highly contended UFC fight is not the right time. My husband is an ex–college athlete and he's really into sports. Though *I* may feel a sense of urgency to vent right then, I've learned to be mindful of more opportune times for me to share so that his attention isn't divided. Using better timing and making a request helps me feel very heard.

Remember, be aware of your voice inflection. Keep it calm and sweet. The right mindset and the right timing are powerful allies to help you recognize situations, in advance, where you otherwise might get triggered, be reactive, or get irritated. There's no need to take it personally or take it as a slight.

Exercise 17.2
Averting Communication Breakdowns

When we're still in our girl, we are more susceptible to being triggered and reactive. The good news is that snipped wires can be repaired and kinks in the wire can be smoothed out. We want to get detoxed so that we can come from a place of responding with poise and maturity.

Step 1: Stop and identify the *real* source or cause of the upset (which may not be an easy task). Ask yourself: What within you got triggered? What were the thoughts that *preceded* the reaction or the triggered feelings?

Step 2: Articulate your upset in Manese. Relationship experts and counselors insist on advising women to "tell him how you feel." *I couldn't disagree with this more!* When you tell him how you feel, you are speaking in Womanese. We will tend to describe the emotional impact of his actions (or inaction). We may say something like, "I'm mad . . . I'm upset . . . I'm angry . . .You hurt my feelings." Yes, this gives a man a "weather report" on your feelings, and cues him that something he did or said *didn't work* for you, but it does *not* mean that he now comprehends what you prefer instead, or knows what would have worked better for you in the situation. So with a man it is *not* useful to just tell him your feelings. He won't know what to do with this.

Step 3: Take it a step further and, in addition to telling him *that* you're upset, also add in *why* it upset you, and last and most important, tell him in Manese (direct, straightforward) what would work better next time.

At this writing, I've been married nearly 21 years, and I *just* learned to speak Manese in the past few years of my marriage. And WOW, what a difference it's made. When a woman learns to speak and understand Manese, as the one who uses five times as many words on a daily basis as a man, the entire level of communication between a couple can experience a quantum leap.

Chapter Eighteen

S = Strengthen
Your "Man-Seasoning" Skills

*In Chapter Eleven, we busted the myth that you
can't change a man. Now we're going to talk about
specific ways to bring about positive change in a man.
I call this ability seasoning.*

Seasoning a man is the ability to positively influence a man in ways
that bring about positive change in him and in how he relates and
engages with you, without defaulting to nagging and complaining.

First, there are several prerequisites for you to have in place in order to
effectively season a man: recognizing that you're the natural leader, continuing to mature, practicing self-care, making the shift to being in your woman,
being serious about developing and bringing forth your feminine leadership
gifts, recognizing the male gifts, and learning to speak Manese and make
requests. Seasoning is a win-win for both of you because your investment
of love, patience, time, and energy refines him, brings out the best in him,
increases his in-tuneness with what works for you, and returns your investment to you ten-fold.

Yes, a man *can* grow, change, mature, and evolve for the better, *if* you
know how to season him.

Interestingly, what most females, in their minds and on their Requirements Lists, are seeking is an *already* seasoned men. We must recognize,
however, that most men are in a raw, unseasoned state—and this includes
married men.

As mentioned earlier in this book, left to the devices of their social conditioning, most men have "pieced together" their relationship knowledge and skills, and their understanding of women, from talk in the locker room, at work, at the bar, or on the sidelines at the sports field. Too often it's based on information gleaned from other confused or misinformed men who also may be wingin' it, or deducing from TV or movies. And to make matters worse, in his previous relationships he's most likely been with females who are in their girl, and thus unfamiliar with how to season a man.

Many of us may, at first, struggle with this concept of seasoning because we can have a condescending attitude about it. We might think of it in terms of it being our *responsibility* or our *burden* as the female. Actually, it's neither of these. The ability to season a man is based on a capacity we have, *by design*, to be natural agents of positive change in our relationships. Thus, wisely and consciously putting our seasoning skills and abilities into action to bring about positive change is a win-win for both of you, and thus the relationship.

Seasoning is most effective when you use repetition to reinforce the desired behaviors. Men are highly seasonable and they respond well to loving seasoning. You season a man in both direct and indirect ways: with your energy field, facial expressions, posture, responses, body language, and communication in the form of your requests, questions, suggestions, loving reminders, and of course, how you inflect your voice (men are very sensitive to this). These all send messages to a man that shape his behavior and responses to you—all of these inform him of what you consider acceptable, pleasing, or allowable in his interactions with you.

To be able to season a man is a skill in and of itself. When seasoning is done from a place of maturity, and from a place of being in your woman, a man responds readily, quickly, and easily.

Remember, a man wants to please a woman he loves or cares about, and he wants to do what pleases her. Seasoning supports this desire in him.

In what instances or situations can seasoning be most useful?

- If you would like him to start or increase a certain behavior (one you desire more of) or stop a behavior (one you want to see less of)
- If you want him to become more aware of what you like, prefer, or what pleases you
- If you desire more of a certain type of loving touch or expressions of affection

- If you want some changes in your sex life
- If you would like him to be more engaged—with you, with the kids (if applicable), in the home (if applicable), in his communication, etc.

The Tools in Your Seasoning Toolbox

Your seasoning toolbox holds the tools you use to season a man. Every woman should have the following in her seasoning toolbox.

Making requests
The ability to comfortably and effectively make a request in Manese is the first tool in your seasoning toolbox. You know you're being effective with your requests when you get your desired response, and it occurs more frequently or consistently.

Here's a little refresher from Chapter Ten on how to make a request. Elements of an effective request:

- It starts with *Would you* or *Will you*, not *Can you*.
- It contains a verb/action.
- It concludes with a question mark.
- It's specific.
- A yes or no response is required.

Making requests enables you to manifest and experience ways of relating that fulfill your heart's desires in your relationship. To illustrate this with a simple example, a few years ago I used my seasoning skills to have my husband begin getting me a certain kind of espresso drink from Starbuck's. How does he now automatically know what I like most, and what to get me, given the myriad of beverage options available at Starbuck's? It started with making a request: "Honey, would you get me my favorite espresso drink from Starbuck's this morning? I'd like a vente, decaf, breve, latte (pronounced *ven-tay, de-caf, brev-ay, lot-ay*).

The first few times I made this request, I wrote it down for him—and he'd take the paper to the Starbuck's counter with him. Each of those first few times he came home with my special espresso drink, he received an enthusiastic and heartfelt thank you, *every* time, along with a kiss or hug (note: this anchored his positive association with fulfilling the desired action). After the first few times, he no longer needed it written down on a piece of paper. Now my husband will often get up on a Saturday morning, make a Starbuck's "run," and surprise me with my favorite Starbuck's espresso drink, while I'm still lounging in bed.

Though we've already discussed making requests in previous chapters, one additional tip: be mindful of making a request and wanting it immediately, but not saying so. Wives, especially, tend to do this with their husbands. Men don't prefer *right now* requests because they could be in the middle of something else, relaxing, or unwinding. They prefer lead time or a timeframe with your requests. Because you put a lot of weight or importance on a particular thing getting done *now*, doesn't mean that he also puts the same weight or importance on it. The key is to resist starting to nag and complain, or going ahead and doing it yourself. *If you do it yourself you are training him to just wait, and let you go ahead and do it.* Is that the behavior you want? I don't think so.

A more effective request regarding the garbage might be, "Honey, would you take out the garbage after you finish watching the game?" Or "Honey, will you take out the garbage tonight before you go to bed?" Remember, he might need a reminder. And not a reminder in that strained, irritated tone of voice that males have come to know oh so well. They hate "that" voice as much as they hate our nagging.

Womanese "conversion"

Your ability to formulate requests is linked to your ability to first relinquish speaking in concepts, a natural tendency when speaking your native tongue of Womanese to other females. You want to develop the skill of being able to "move aside" the concept and clearly and directly articulate what you want to have actually occur, in literal terms, often in verbs. This is a second tool to have in your seasoning toolbox. To be a good seasoner, you want to be able to readily convert Womanese into Manese. These next few tips will aid you in conversion basics, so that you can begin applying and practicing Manese in your relationships, and thus strengthening your seasoning skills. Practice is the key.

When females use conceptual words and phrases, men struggle to understand what we really mean. To their ears, our concepts sound vague, general, and open to a wide range of interpretation. So we get to drill down and get to what the concept is actually describing, and then articulate it simply and directly in Manese.

Below is a list of some classic Womanese "concept" words that we tend to use in our love relationships communication. These are the types of phrases we're comfortable and familiar with and work just fine in our communication with other females. When using these *same* concepts with men, however, they create confusion for them and frustration for you.

Support	Work more as a team	Better . . .
Intimacy	Help out	Grow/grow together
Communication	Quality time	Next level
Affectionate	More . . .	Connected

In my *For Married Women Only* tele-seminar, we have a chance to practice our Womanese-to-Manese conversion skills.

On one tele-seminar call, I did a role play with Andrice, one of the participants. I asked her to think of something she wanted "more of" from her husband (most wives can come up with this in a split second). She immediately said, "More affection." I then asked her to think about what this would look like if "more affection" were happening in the way that she desired and taking place in the way that worked for her. She said, "He'd hold my hand more."

I then said, "Okay, so now I want you to be even *more* specific, though I know that you *already* think that you're being specific." Andrice started to laugh, because that's exactly what she was thinking, and so were the other wives on the line. She replied, "I would like him to hold my hand when we're out on a date, when we're walking to and from the car, and also when we're in the movies." "Perfect," I said. I then reminded her that if she was thinking that this level of detail was overkill, unnecessary, and should be obvious to him, this was a remnant of her H.S.A.K. Love Lie thinking. If you want to communicate in a way that enables you to more likely receive (not get, but receive) what you want from him, then you want to be able to speak your request in Manese.

Andrice was then ready to practice articulating her actual request. Her practice request was: "Honey, while we're in a movie, and when we're walking to and from the car on our date nights, would you hold my hand?"

The better you get at being able to convert these Womanese types of words and concepts into direct, literal, actionable Manese language, the sooner you can begin to experience the incredible benefits of being bilingual and him not just hearing you but *comprehending* what you are communicating to him. Most important, once he's clear about what you're asking of him, he can readily respond, and usually does. Being bilingual and speaking Manese supports more peace and better communication flow, supports you getting what you want, and with less friction and less stress for both of you.

Now it's your turn to practice strengthening your seasoning skills by (1) converting your communication from Womanese to Manese and (2) formulating a request.

Exercise 18.1
Converting from Womanese to Manese

Step 1: Think about three things that you want "more of" in your relationship. Write them here.

1. _____
2. _____
3. _____

Step 2: Think more deeply about what you are using this concept to describe—what would actually be going on, right now, if it were happening? Get "beneath" the concept, "peel it back," and zero in on *what would be actually happening if the "more of" were occurring?* Don't rush. Be clear, be specific, and use verbs (action words).

For example, if you wrote down the word "support," what does "support" look like in practice and demonstration? *What actions would actually be taking place if "more support" were occurring right now, live, in real time?* Please describe each concept from your "more of" list in terms of what it would look like in practice and demonstration.

1. _____
2. _____
3. _____

Step 3: You are now going to use what you wrote here to help convert your communications to a request in Manese. Then you'll be ready to speak your request, live, and in real time. Another way to come at this is to ask: *What would I be observing if this "concept" was taking place, live, and in real time, right now?* Now convert each of the actions described in Step 2 into a request.

1. Would you/Will you_____?
2. Would you/Will you_____?
3. Would you/Will you_____?

T.E.L.L. Him

When you see a desired behavior exhibited, you want to use positive reinforcement to clearly let him know that you were pleased by his particular action. This is the third tool in your seasoning toolbox. Thus, when a request is fulfilled or honored, or he does something that pleases you, it is important that you T.E.L.L. Him:

T = Thank him
E = Express delight and pleasure
L = Let him know that you appreciate it (this may include lovingly touching him)
L = Let him know why you appreciate it (be short, sweet, and to the point)

The same way that we never get tired of compliments, a man never tires of you "T.E.L.L.-ing" him. Nothing is too small or insignificant to apply the T.E.L.L. Him principle.

In the Love Academy, married women especially argue this point. *"Well, I don't get any thanks for all of the things I do. Why do I have to say thank you when he doesn't thank me?"* My straightforward answer: *Because it works for the male spirit.* This is a sufficiently compelling reason. This does not mean that males don't have some serious areas for growth and improvement, too, nor does this excuse them from learning to do what works for the female spirit. (That's another book though.) Just so you know that I keep things fair in my Men-tality 101 seminars with the gents, the men often ask, "But why should I have to do that?" and my response is often: *Because it works for the female spirit.* I may then ask, "Gentlemen, are you more interested in being right, or in doing what works?" This usually brings the questioning to an end.

Speaking appreciation

There is a difference between speaking appreciation and saying "thank you." Thank you is said after a man completes a task or action, no matter how small. Because he is feat-oriented, and completing a task is the completion of a feat—even if it is a small feat like taking out the garbage—saying thank you carries more weight for men than you may know. Speaking appreciation, however, goes beyond saying thank you and addresses his essence, qualities, and/or character. Think of him as a water pitcher. Rarely do we stop to speak appreciation into a man. When you speak appreciation into him, it is like pouring water into him. It fills and feeds his male spirit. This is a fourth tool for your seasoning toolbox.

For example, if my husband were sitting in front of me right now, here are the kinds of things I might speak *into* him about, preferably in person. I'd look him in the eyes and say, "Honey, I appreciate . . . your humor and laughter, your warm hugs, your huge smile, how relaxed you remain even when I get all worked up, your sparkling eyes, your consistently positive demeanor, your easy-going manner, your smart decision-making, how sexy you are to me, your entrepreneurial spirit, and your soft, juicy lips."

I can't emphasize this enough: men never tire of hearing "thank you," and *especially* being on the receiving end of a woman he loves or cares for speaking appreciation "into his spirit." This also applies to our sons and other males in our lives. Speaking appreciation is an essential man-seasoning tool. The more you practice it, the more he opens himself up to you. The more open and responsive he is to you, the more he wants to please you and see you pleased.

But first, before you are able to speak appreciation into his spirit, you have to zero in on attributes, qualities, and characteristics that you consider admirable in him. Remember, these are separate from his actions, tasks, or the things he does. Last, treat "speaking appreciation" as if it were "liquid love" you are pouring into his ears, and filling him up like water fills up a pitcher. Let's practice.

Exercise 18.2
Speaking Appreciation

Step 1: Think of a significant male in your life. If you're in a relationship, choose your husband/boyfriend/partner. Otherwise, you can choose your father, son, male relative, male coworker, or boss, if applicable. Think about his essence, his character, his spirit, his being, and list at least three qualities you appreciate about him here:

1. _____
2. _____
3. _____

Step 2: Make or seize an opportunity to speak appreciation into him. (Key word: Speak) Speaking appreciation is from *your* mouth to *his* ear. This is opposed to texting, emailing, or writing it. First you want to get familiar and comfortable with verbally speaking appreciation, and later, you can add in texting, emailing, or writing it. The most powerful form is to speak it, however. When you speak appreciation, you can start your sentence with a very simple lead-in statement: "I appreciate . . ." or, "What I appreciate about you is . . ."

Manese—some bonus seasoning tips

Okay, we've laid some good groundwork about the basics of seasoning a man. Here are a few other things to be mindful of that will support you in being a good seasoner.

1. Men are emotional, too, but have been socialized not to broadcast and process their emotions verbally, especially within love relationships. For example, instead of asking, "So how do you feel about this?" Ask: "So what do you think about this?" or "What are your thoughts on this?" Instead of, "What do you feel I should do?" Ask: "What do you think I should do?"

2. Be very mindful of the female gift of voice inflection—the unique way your voice rises and falls, even within the same word. Most of us use it to our detriment instead of to our advantage.

3. In an area where he feels he has expertise, has it handled, or is capable of handling it, having you try to tell him what to do or to offer your "two cents" is highly irritating. Refrain from doing this.

4. Refrain from giving a man a long list of things to do (more than four items is long to him). It can overwhelm him. As females we can process and execute multiple tasks at once, but this tends not to be the case with men. Their gift is a single point of focus at a time, while ours is multiple points of focus at a time. Limit your list to two items at a time (yes, two), and then once he completes those two, you can give him two more. Resist the inclination to interpret this as "bad' or wrong because it's different from how we are able to complete five tasks, at once, and all within the same amount of time.

5. This tip is worth repeating since I know that it can be a stickler: Once you've asked him to do something or told him what you need him to do (in Manese), don't succumb to the temptation to go ahead and do it yourself or arrange for someone else to do it after you've asked him to. *Otherwise, you're training him to disregard your requests and to be less and less engaged.*

6. When you're lovingly reminding him of something, state it based upon the affirmative action you desire from him. Instead of saying, "Don't forget to take out the garbage," affirmatively say, "Please remember to take out the garbage before you come to bed." This puts the focus on the desired behavior instead of on the undesirable behavior.

Maureen's story

Maureen, single, age 34, a Love Academy 101 and 201 graduate and also a private coaching client, shares her experience with men before and after learning how to season a man.

Before Love Academy, plenty of men had come into my life, but time after time, the relationships were very short-lived, sex-based, and unfulfilling. I continued to attract unavailable, noncommittal men and I would use sex to try to keep them around, but it never worked. I would then get hurt, defensive, and combative. I had my heart broken so many times.

During the forgiveness process in Love Academy 201, I was able to release this long-held belief, and the rage toward my father, my ex-boyfriend (the father of my child), and self-hatred that had lived in my body for so long. My heart is no longer laden with sadness, hurt, and resentment.

I am now in a new relationship, unlike any other I've been in before. I have shed a lot of my "girlish" ways, stepped into being in my woman, learned how to lead, speak Manese, and season a man. Thank goodness that I'm no longer operating from the Requirements List Love Lie, or I would have screened and rejected this wonderful man right out of my life, before getting to know him since he makes less money than me right now. My radiance is on, and I am clear in my communication now. I state exactly what action I want him to take through making a request. He agrees readily. I previously suffered from the H.S.A.K. Syndrome, assuming that a guy knew what I liked or didn't like. Now I act from the assumption that he doesn't know. I now let him know, and lovingly. And when he does or says things that I would love more of, I use the T.E.L.L. Him approach. I sincerely thank him immediately, and I sometimes add in a hug or a loving stroke on his arm. I also use another man-seasoning tool, speaking appreciation. I share with him the great things I see in him.

I feel truly loved, adored, appreciated, protected, safe, trusting, and deeply satisfied and fulfilled in a relationship with a man, for the first time in my life. I'm so excited; we are talking about getting engaged to be married!

Chapter Nineteen

S = **Seek** Healing and Forgiveness

*This chapter covers the crucial divine self-work
that directly impacts your relationship with yourself
and your emotional healing.*

This chapter could also be called the liberation chapter because we're talking about learning to heal and set yourself free from emotional baggage from your past, emotional baggage you may not even be aware that you're still carrying.

Healing and Forgiveness

Nelson Mandela, national hero imprisoned for 27 years and former president of South Africa, is quoted as saying, "Resentment is like drinking poison and then hoping that it will kill your enemies." Who it can slowly kill is us—in the form of stress, anxiety, and eventually, the manifestation of physical dis-ease in our bodies, if the resentment is harbored for long enough.

Too often we talk about needing to forgive, but we don't really know how to do it, or we've done it only partially. Forgiveness, when it is done as a comprehensive process, "clears" from your system the negative emotions and emotional residue from your past that are creating blockages, hindrances, *in present* time.

Partial forgiveness is like being partially pregnant. Either you've forgiven or you haven't. It is not a partial process. We may have burdensome, toxic, or damaging "emotional baggage" that we are still carrying around from past situations or relationships, and this includes emotional baggage from our parent-child relationship, whether both parents were present in the home or not.

You know you're not healed if you keep creating what Joan Gattuso, in her book *A Course in Love*, calls "the same old misery again." You must get to the underlying cause. When we are unhealed, she explains, "We pretend that we have nothing to do with what shows up in our lives….We project what is really our own negative baggage 'out there' somewhere, not recognizing it when it boomerangs and hits us in the face." We may lament, she explains, "It's happening because of an inner core belief that you deserve to be dumped on, to be used, and thrown away," and I might add, and because you feel unworthy of better. She reminds us, "You are not at fault, but you are wounded." The forgiveness process is a spiritual and emotional process that has the ability to heal these emotional wounds and dismantle the mechanism that has you getting hit with this "boomeranging baggage," and continuing to attract unhealthy, abusive, or negative patterns in your relationships.

In this chapter, I am going to provide you with the steps for moving through an actual forgiveness process that will begin to heal and liberate you from old emotional baggage. Forgiveness is 1) an essential part of your detox process, 2) an essential step in shifting out of being in your girl to being in your woman, and 3) part of your preparation for attracting healthy love. Forgiveness results in emotional and spiritual freedom.

I'd read many books that included sections on forgiveness; heard pastors speak about the importance of forgiveness; participated in exercises; spoken about it for years; led others through forgiveness exercises in my courses; and wrote about it in my first two books, *Sacred Pampering Principles*, and *All the Joy You Can Stand*, years prior. But it was going to be new for me to do forgiveness work in the midst of my marriage crisis after four years of trying to save it—when my bitterness, resentment, and resignation were at their highest point. In my mind, up to that point, the finger was pointed at my husband. After all, *he* was the one who needed to "get his act together," so I thought. So *me* personally doing some forgiveness work hadn't occurred to me.

If I hadn't said yes to forgiveness in my marriage, my marriage wouldn't exist today; and neither would the Love Academy nor this book. I remember another fateful moment in this journey when my dad said to me, at one of my highest points of frustration, "Debrena, there's only one place left for you to turn in your situation—*forgiveness*. You can't undo the past, but you can undo the emotional damage of the past." I knew he was right. I had not yet begun my forgiveness work, which didn't yet include this process with the newly inserted step I'm sharing with you here. After all of the appointments, counseling sessions, and conversations my husband and I'd had, the "heart work" still hadn't been addressed. We both were still operating on top of feelings of anger, resentment, betrayal, and distrust, and our hearts weren't reopened to each other.

Little did I know that, down the road, two years later, new "spiritual downloads, " this time related to the forgiveness process, were coming, ones that were going to take my understanding of forgiveness to a new level, enabling me to teach an even more powerful and potent process to others than what I had personally used in my own personal detox process.

The Dawn of a New Forgiveness Process

Two years after my personal detox process had completed and my marriage was restored and transformed, I was scheduled to lead my first-ever Love Academy 201 Advanced Course in California. I'd been leading Love Academy 101 courses for seven months already, and I knew that I wanted to have a live, real-time, facilitated group-forgiveness process be part of the Advanced Course's curriculum. It was the "release it and let it go" approach to forgiveness work I'd been teaching for years that I planned to use. This approach consisted of acknowledging what happened in the past that is causing the emotional pain, acknowledging who you perceive as causing the emotional pain, acknowledging the emotions, and then making the decision to "release it and let it go."

There's a lot of conversation about the need to forgive when it comes to relationships, but it often remains as only a conversation where people don't know how to engage in an actual forgiveness process and would really appreciate some guidance. The Love Academy 201 Advanced Course was designed to address both of these.

During this inaugural session of the 201 Advanced Course intensive, after the lunch break, the focus shifted to leading the group through the written portion of the forgiveness process together. The exercise got underway with each participant finding a quiet corner of the room and completing her reflections and writing portion of the exercise.

As I was sitting patiently and quietly, waiting for participants to complete the writing portion of the forgiveness process, God chose this moment to let me know that He was going to introduce me to a new step in the forgiveness process I'd been teaching for years. God said, "*Do you know that there's another step to this process? You have them releasing the energy of their emotions before it's been transformed.*"

As you can imagine, I was stunned. I couldn't believe that another download was coming at this moment, in the middle of the Advanced course. But I was listening. He certainly had my attention. If all of the women weren't already deeply engrossed in their own reflecting and writing exercise, they would have looked up to see with some very interesting facial expressions on my face. It was hard for me to believe I was "hearing" this because I had assumed that my Love Lies download several years earlier was going to be it. I didn't anticipate that I'd ever receive another download of that caliber.

He continued, "*The energy I brought into existence when I created the world is still completely available. Energy is able to be transformed, transmuted, or transferred, but not created or destroyed.* (I recognized this part—it's the scientific basis of the Third Law of Thermodynamics). *Therefore the energy in each of the "negative" emotions that you're planning to have the participants release needs to be transformed **first**. Right now, you're planning to have them release it in the same energetic form in which it already exists. You want to help them transform it to its next higher level. Otherwise, it's like tossing away an acorn without ever setting free the mighty oak that lives within it. Today, and going forward, you're going to add an additional step that will support participants in transforming the "negative" emotional energy from their past into a much higher and elevated level of positive emotional energy.*"

Time seemed to slow down. Everything seemed to fade into a background blur as I was listening with my inner spiritual ears. It was clear that God wanted me to integrate a new step into the process today, during this session. "Okay, so what do you want me to do right now?" I asked. "They've already started their exercise, and I've already given them the instructions for the rest of the steps in the process. Can you at least give me a metaphor to use when we reconvene to make it easier for me to share this new insight you've given me about forgiveness?"

Before I could barely finish formulating that last thought, a vision popped into my head that made it crystal clear for me. Imagine a woman in a jail cell, an old-fashioned jail cell with the widely spaced black bars, like the ones you see in the old cowboy Westerns. This is a single jail cell with a cot in the corner. She's pacing anxiously back and forth. There is a deputy outside the jail cell with a key hanging from his belt—a long, large, black skeleton-bone-style key.

She keeps looking at one key hanging on his belt loop, as she continues to pace back and forth. You can see and sense her growing anxiety. She is getting more and more agitated as she perceives him as holding the key to her freedom.

In a moment of exasperation, she thrusts her hand into her pocket and, surprised, finds a key in it. She pulls out the key, examines it, and realizes that it's a copy of the same key hanging on the deputy's belt loop. All of this time, she thought that the deputy held the key to her freedom, while it was within her reach the entire time. The woman then walks over to the door of her cell, reaches between the widely spaced bars with the key in her hand, inserts the key into the lock, and then turns it. Click. The lock clicks open.

Now imagine the woman pulling the key out of the lock, pulling her arm from between the bars, and then pushing open the door to her jail cell. The door slowly swings open wide. The woman steps forward, crosses over the threshold between bondage and freedom, and steps out her jail cell to freedom. "*Now she's finally free,*" God says to me.

He went on, "*So how many steps are involved in this process, based upon this vision I gave you?*" I reviewed the process in my mind again.

1. In the vision, the woman first had to realize that the key to her jail cell was in her pocket the whole time she'd been fretting and pacing back and forth.
2. Once she recognized that she had the key, she then had to decide to use it.
3. Then she had to insert the key into the lock and turn the key.
4. She then had to push the door open.
5. Last, she had to walk across the threshold and out of her jail cell, to freedom.

"Five steps," I answered. "*Correct,*" God responded. "*And the complete forgiveness process that I want you to start teaching, right here, right now today, in this course is now going to include a total of five steps.*"

This "transform the energy" step, which is the equivalent of step five in the jail cell example, has been missing. Remember, energy is neither created nor destroyed, it just changes form. Too many have stopped at step 4—they've swung open the door and stood there, or taken a few steps toward the open door, and they equate that with being free. The original form of the emotional energy is still intact. This final step to be added, changing the form of the emotional energy, has been missing. You must walk across the threshold before truly being free and out of the jail cell. It's this new fifth step, this critical, transformative step, that is be added, so that the forgiveness process can truly liberate you.

What's important to know here is that, in this vision, the woman wasn't free until she crossed the threshold. Realizing she had the key didn't set her free. Unlocking the jail cell and pushing the door open didn't mean she was free. It's not until she walked across the threshold that she was truly free. Most of us have *started* the forgiveness process but we haven't finished it. The key's been turned in the lock and the door has been pushed open. Or the door's been pushed open but we have not yet crossed the threshold to freedom.

When we all reconvened, I shared this jail cell metaphor to help the participants understand the relevance and impact of the new "updated" forgiveness process I was going to be sharing with them, and how it would help us experience even greater emotional freedom. They got it. They understood. And the results were remarkable and life-changing for each participant. You may have taken yourself through a forgiveness process before, and most likely, this "transform the energy" step was not a part of your process. Here you will have the opportunity to include it in your process.

At the end of the five-step process, the womens' appearances had literally changed. They looked different. Faces were radiant and relaxed; eyes were shining; bodies were relaxed, shoulders had dropped; tension in facial muscles had eased; women were smiling; they looked released and free. Through tears of relief and joy, one participant remarked that this five-part forgiveness process felt more liberating for her than the five years of therapy she'd been receiving. Incredible. Amazing.

Now It's Your Turn

In this section, we're also going to move through the five-part forgiveness process, but here I'm adapting it specifically around healing past experiences that are directly affecting how we're relating and engaging in our love relationships. For optimal impact, this comprehensive five-part forgiveness process is best done in a group. But it can also be done with two or three others, if possible, or at a Vitamin D Gathering. Moving through this process with others is even more powerful than doing it solo.

If you're human, you probably have some regrets and disappointments you're holding against yourself. And whether you're aware of it or not, it's likely that you've caused other people in your life pain, hurt, inconvenience, heartache, setbacks, and/or disappointment—whether knowingly or unknowingly. So the need for forgiveness of yourself applies as well. Instead of being stuck in the jail cell of condemnation, judgment, rejection, unworthiness, self-loathing, blame, guilt, or shame, you have a way out: forgiveness.

A Course in Miracles, one of the most profound and potent spiritual development books I've encountered, explains that forgiveness is "an opportunity to let perceptions be healed and errors be corrected." In Lesson 46 of the course, it shares, "Those who forgive are releasing themselves from illusions. . . . Fear condemns and love forgives." Forgiveness returns you to your natural state of joy—a state that enables you to experience love, channel love, and be love. *Yesss!*

Dr. Christiane Northrup, in her wellness work with women, shares how many women think that "forgiving someone who hurt you is the same as saying that what happened to you was okay, and that it didn't hurt you. Nothing could be further from the truth. . . . Forgiveness doesn't mean that what happened to you was okay. It means that you are no longer willing to allow that experience to adversely affect your life. Forgiveness is something we do, ultimately for ourselves." I couldn't agree more. Forgiveness is one of the most gracious gifts you can give yourself.

Remember, this forgiveness process is *not* a one-time event. Given the years of build-up of toxic emotional junk, funk, and gunk from past relationships, *once is not enough.* This process should be applied periodically, every six months. I repeat, this process should *not be a one-time occurrence.* It is important that you recognize this and plan to revisit it every six months.

Preparation

This entire five-part process involves some basic supplies, and the appropriate time and space to complete it. I recommend that you give yourself an interrupted block of 90 minutes. You want to be in a place where you have some privacy since there are statements you're going to be reading out loud. You want to be able to do this without holding back or being concerned about someone overhearing you. It's important that you follow and complete the full process, step-by-step. All you'll need is your worksheet and a pen or pencil and a tissue. The tissue is to wipe healing tears that may flow.

This process involves focusing on five people to forgive at a time. The first three slots are pre-assigned. Your own name goes at the top of the list, followed by your father and then your mother, even if both or either of them is deceased, or were not present or active in your life. You don't have to use their formal first names but can use Mom/Mother/Mama or Dad/Father/Daddy, whichever applies to you.

Healing parent wounds

In *Intimate Communion*, David Deida, transformational author and teacher, gives us insight into a fascinating phenomenon that occurs between child and parent, and thus the reason parents are near the top of the forgiveness list. He explains, "Whatever our parents didn't give us enough of (love, attention, praise, freedom, etc.), is exactly the thing we will not get from our romantically chosen partner." He calls this your "childhood imprint."

This may seem like a strange correlation when you first read it. Deida goes on to illuminate what feeds this dynamic. "Our new partner seems so special because we unconsciously hope to . . . finally get the love we always wanted, the acceptance we always desired, the fulfillment of our heart that we always craved. And because we have unconsciously chosen our parents in our partner, we have chosen someone who will *not* give us what we always wanted, in exactly the same way that our parents didn't." He continues, "Even if our romantic partner gives us what we want, we often cannot receive it, because our childhood imprint doesn't believe it is real."

Another perspective on this phenomenon is given by psychotherapist and author Ken Page when he explains, "Unconsciously, we're most attracted to people who can wound us in just the same way we were wounded in our childhood . . . our conscious self is drawn to the positive qualities we yearn for, but our unconscious draws us to the qualities which hurt us the most as children. The child in us believes that if our current replacements for the original perpetrators would finally change their minds, apologize, or make up for their terrible rupture of trust, we can escape from our prison of unworthiness."

Now, your experience with your parents may not have been this traumatic, at least at first glance, and you may even consider yourself having a positive and healthy relationship with your parents. Nonetheless, your relationship with your parents serves as your first human relationship and acts as a template for you—even if one or both were absent or deceased, or you were raised by someone else. Even if your relationship with your parents was fundamentally good, there are most likely some unconscious beliefs adopted or conclusions drawn at a young age from what you observed or heard in your household about love and relationships. And actually, if you're human, and as a natural by-product of interacting with other humans, there is forgiveness work to be done—forgiveness of self and/or forgiveness of others.

The forgiveness process can also help heal unconscious beliefs and the Love Lies that may have affected you in past relationships, or in current or future relationships, as well as other emotional baggage that you may unknowingly be carrying around. Here's a synopsis of the steps of the process.

Step 1: *Realize.* Forgiveness is a conscious decision. Remember, the woman in the jail cell first had to realize she had the key in her pocket. She had to realize that she held the key to her own freedom.

Step 2: *Decide and Identify.* Decide to use the key. She could have chosen to leave the key in her pocket and stay in jail. In addition to deciding to forgive, in this step you also decide on the names of the two other individuals, in addition to yourself and your parents, that you're going to focus on for your five-step process.

Step 3: *Make the Connection.* Identify the specific situations, incidents, or circumstances with regard to that person that caused you an upset, or to feel offended, violated, or betrayed, and the emotions associated with the incidences. This could be a situation where you were yelled at, embarrassed, wrongfully accused of something, treated unfairly, violated physically or sexually, or abused, for example. For the forgiveness work with yourself, it could be choices, decisions, behaviors, actions taken, or reactions from your past where you are still holding regret, disappointment, anger, guilt, or shame toward yourself. This step equates to the woman putting the key into the lock and turning it.

Step 4: *Acknowledge the Emotions.* When you read your statements out loud, you are able to more fully acknowledge the emotions and begin loosening their grip on you. It's like throwing open the door to the jail cell and acknowledging those emotions have been keeping you locked in.

Step 5: *Transform the Old Emotions and Embrace the New Emotions.* From the seed or core emotional energy of the negative, low-vibration emotion is birthed the transformed, positive, higher-vibration emotion. Transform the old and embrace the new by naming and declaring the transformed emotion. This is much like an oak tree being birthed from an acorn seed, or a caterpillar transforming to emerge as a butterfly. Using the jail cell metaphor, this is related to walking across the threshold, from bondage into freedom.

In most other forgiveness processes, we've been attempting to release the energy of negative emotions too soon, before we've broken open the "seed" the negative emotion represents and set the new, positive emotion free. We've been releasing the emotion before we've had the opportunity to transmute it into its higher form by speaking forth the new state of being into existence. You have to cross the threshold, which represents transforming and upgrading the low-level energy of the negative emotion to the higher-level energy of the positive emotion.

Miss this step and you miss the learning and insight that is to come with your forgiveness process, and how the experience related to your personal soul development. Miss this step and the positive emotions that exist, in potential, within the negative emotion, are never "set free," birthed, and transmitted. It is the equivalent of the acorn never setting the oak tree free or the chrysalis never setting the butterfly free.

In *Zero Limits*, author Joe Vitale describes an ancient Hawaiian healing system he studied that had a similar basis. He explains, "LOVE begins the mystical process of transmuting the erroneous thoughts. In this spiritual correction process, LOVE first neutralizes the erroneous emotions . . . . In the next step, LOVE then releases the neutralized energies from the thoughts, leaving them in a state of . . . true freedom."

With regard to emotional baggage from your past, to "let go" means to relinquish your grip and release the emotion because you see no further need for it. Once the oak tree starts to germinate, it releases itself from the acorn seed and the acorn seed is left behind. Once the butterfly emerges and releases itself from the chrysalis, the chrysalis is left behind.

Exercise 19.1
The Five-Part Forgiveness Process

Read the following statements out loud and slowly in preparation for beginning your process and more deeply understanding the power of forgiveness.

When I Forgive . . .

I give up (yield, give up possession of) the grudge (a deep-seated feeling of resentment).

I give up the "attack" (condemnation, projecting anger) on either myself or others.

I give up the grievances (causes of distress resulting in complaint or resistance).

I give up the "make wrong" (blame, condemnation) of myself or others.

I choose to yield the anger, resentment, hurt, pain, and condemnation in exchange for restoration and the unblocked and unimpeded flow of joy and love energy.

I initiate movement of the frozen, stagnant, or hardened energies of fear, guilt, grief, or shame.

Overview of the Steps for Completing the Worksheet

Step 1: List five people (remember: you first, followed by your mom and dad, and then two others) you are choosing to forgive.

1. _____
2. _____
3. _____
4. _____
5. _____

Step 2: Each of the five names you listed will have their *own* designated paragraph. One name per paragraph. In the first portion of the paragraph identify the hurtful or painful situation(s) or incident(s) that caused you to write down this person's name.

Step 3: In the second portion of the paragraph acknowledge and describe the emotions associated with the situation or incidence.

Step 4: After you have completed all five paragraphs *and* the additional step for each parent, read each completed paragraph *out loud*, and read the right column of your parent statements (I now choose to give myself more . . .). Slowly and out loud please. This is very important.

Step 5: Declare the old emotion you're releasing, and the new, transformed emotion and way of being that you're embracing. Then declare what you are going to be giving "more of" to yourself, going forward.

Before beginning, find a comfortable, private, and undisturbed place in which to do this reflecting and writing exercise. I recommend that you have several tissues on-hand in case some healing tears start to flow. I don't want you to have to interrupt your process to get up to get tissue once you've started the exercise.

Step 1 in the Forgiveness Process

1. (Myself) I now choose to forgive myself for (list incidents and situations that you perceive caused you hurt; unnecessary suffering; to make a poor, wrong, or bad choice; or caused you difficulty or for what you failed to do, or failed to do adequately) . . . Name a few key incidents. _____

_____

This made me feel (name the specific emotions associated with these incidents)
_____
_____

I now choose to let go of my resentment/pain/hurt/self-condemnation, and/or my bitterness. I now choose to move out of bondage and back into freedom. I now bless myself. I release myself and set myself free!

Step 2 in the Forgiveness Process

2. (Parent) I now choose to forgive (insert "Dad/Father/Daddy") _____
for (incidents and situations where I perceive that he caused me hurt/pain/
unnecessary suffering/wronged me/betrayed, rejected, or abandoned me/or
failed me) . . . Name a few key incidents. _____

_____

This made me feel . . . (name the specific emotions) _____
_____

I now choose to let go of my resentment/pain/anger/hurt/rage/blame/bitter-
ness. I now choose to move out of bondage and back into freedom.

I now bless (insert Dad/Father/Daddy) _____

I release (insert Dad/Father/Daddy)_____ and set myself free!

Additional Question for the Parent Exercise:
What did I most yearn for/long for from him that I feel I didn't fully receive?
(be specific) _____
_____

Step 3 in the Forgiveness Process

3. (Parent) I now choose to forgive (insert Mom/Mother/Mama) _____
for (incidents and situations where I perceive that she caused me hurt/pain/
unnecessary suffering/wronged me/betrayed, rejected, or abandoned me/or
failed me) . . . Name a few key incidents. _____
_____

This made me feel . . . (name the specific emotions) _____
_____

I now choose to let go of my resentment/pain/anger/hurt/rage/blame/bitter-
ness. I now choose to move out of bondage and back into freedom.

I now bless (insert Mom/Mother/Mama) _____

I release (insert Mom/Mother/Mama) _____ and set myself free!

Additional Question for the Parent Exercise:
What did I most yearn for/long for from him that I feel I didn't fully receive?
(be specific) _____
_____

Step 4 in the Forgiveness Process

4. (4th person) I now choose to forgive (insert name) _____
for (incidents and situations where I perceive that you caused me hurt/pain/
unnecessary suffering/wronged me/betrayed, rejected, or abandoned me/or
failed me) . . . Name a few key incidents. _____
_____

This made me feel . . . (name the specific emotions) _____
_____

I now choose to let go of my resentment/pain/anger/hurt/rage/blame/bitter-
ness. I now choose to move out of bondage and back into freedom.

I now bless (insert their name) _____

I release (insert their name) _____ and set myself free!

Step 5 in the Forgiveness Process

5. (5th person) I now choose to forgive (insert name)_____
for (incidents and situations where I perceive that you caused me hurt/pain/
wronged me/betrayed, rejected, or abandoned me/or failed me) . . . Name a few
key incidents. _____
_____

This made me feel . . . (name the specific emotions) _____
_____

I now choose to let go of my resentment/pain/anger/hurt/rage/blame/ bitterness. I now choose to move out of bondage and back into freedom.

I now bless (insert their name) _____

I release (insert their name) _____ and set myself free!

5A. Now, take the words you listed in the "This made me feel" section of the
    paragraph and write them in the left-hand column of your worksheet
    chart (one per line).

5B. After listing the emotions in the left column, you're going to think of a word
    that is the *emotional opposite* of the word you wrote in the left column.
    Think carefully about this. Write each opposite emotion in the right-hand
    column, directly across from its corresponding left-hand column word.
    Use a dictionary if you need to, so that you're aware of the accurate defi-
    nitions of certain emotions. In the right column, avoid using opposites
    that are simply the same word with "un" removed (i.e., unworthy/worthy,
    unlovable/loveable).

Emotions: I Now Release Feeling . . . Then Take a Breath	I Now Claim and Embrace Being . . .

You are now going to be speaking out loud. Before you do, read the directions carefully and be sure you are clear about how to read your statement out loud correctly.

These are the two statements you'll need to read out loud, for each line:

I now release feeling _____ (insert the
     word from the left hand column) . . . **then take a slow, d-e-e-e-p breath. . . .**
I now claim and embrace being _____
     (insert the word from the right-hand column).
You're going to speak these statements out loud for each line.

5C. *Additional Parent Exercise:* List the words vertically that you wrote in *both*
     the additional parent exercises from paragraphs two and three (combine
     into one vertical list). You will then insert the words into the statements in
     the right column.

Out loud, you're now going to read each of the completed statements in
the right-column.

What I most yearned for/longed for that I feel that I didn't fully get . . . (list each of the words from both additional parent exercises)	What I now get to give to myself (Insert the word from the left column into the blank in the right column statement and read the statement)
	I now choose to give to myself more
	I now choose to give to myself more
	I now choose to give to myself more
	I now choose to give to myself more

Once you've completed all five steps of the process, sit quietly and complete the reflection questions in exercise 19.2.

Exercise 19.2
Forgiveness Process: Reflections and Reflection Questions

Consider this: Every life experience, even the most difficult, has value that can move us onward, upward, and forward in our personal spiritual development and soul growth. When you move through the final two steps of the five-step forgiveness process, you will see for yourself how the emotional energy of what you may have initially perceived as only negative, toxic, undesirable, or unwanted, is like an acorn seed that, when transformed, bursts open to release the mighty oak it holds inside. If you label the acorn (the negative emotion) as having no value, as needing to be discarded or released immediately, you never crack open the acorn shell. This encased emotion needs to be birthed to support you as you continue to grow, develop, learn, and move forward in fulfillment of your life mission/assignment.

If you're born onto Planet Earth, you can count on having experiences that involve the universal human themes of pain, hurt, disappointment, suffering, fear, loss, gain, death, victory, overcoming, defeat, trust, distrust, betrayal, fear, insecurity, judgment, and inadequacy, to name a few. Consider that those who show up in your life through your most significant experiences have the potential to be your greatest teachers. Through the forgiveness process, we're able to see more clearly how the people who have caused us the most hurt, pain, and disappointment are often the bringers of our deepest lessons that grow us the most. While challenging situations and incidences were occurring, we didn't realize that the most difficult folks in our lives, including parents or family members, were possibly our greatest teachers.

The emotions that you wrote on the right side of the final page of your forgiveness worksheet capture the "lessons" that are especially for you and your soul's development. When you look at the right-hand column, what are the "soul lesson" themes that personally emerge for you?

_____

_____

_____

_____

_____

_____

_____

_____

_____

The forgiveness test with others

Participants in my courses often ask, "So how do I know if I've truly forgiven someone?" A great way to test to see if you're "cleared" of regret, shame, anger, guilt, embarrassment, condemnation, or judgment from your past with the other individuals mentioned on your list is to ask yourself these questions: Would you be comfortable and at ease sitting at a dinner table where this person was present? You can also apply the "what-if-he/she-walked-in-the-room-right-now" test. If that person were to walk in the room, what would be the effect upon you? Would there be any bodily response—nervousness, nausea, anger, clenching your jaw, stomach flips, or heart racing—or would you be relaxed and at ease? If you have a reaction such as those mentioned, then your forgiveness process with that person is not yet complete. There's still more or deeper forgiveness work to do. You haven't yet fully "cleared" the old emotional residue from your system.

The forgiveness test with yourself

You also can test to find out if your emotional residue in the form of regret, anger, guilt, shame, disappointment, or self-condemnation is cleared. Imagine that you are among a group of people and you are asked to share publicly. If you are able to publicly share about the incidents, scenarios, and happenings from your past that gave rise to the regret, anger, guilt, shame, disappointment, or self-condemnation without feeling any twinges of them in your gut or physical reactions in your body, then you have cleared them. Remember, forgiveness is not a one-time event, but an ongoing process I recommend revisiting every six months.

Forgiveness enabled me to begin re-opening my heart to my husband, through gritted teeth at first, and insisting that he should be the one to make the first move and re-open his heart first, not me. Though we'd been working on our marriage for a few years at that point, it hadn't yet involved forgiveness work. I still harbored hurt, disgust, and anger toward him. During the forgiveness process, the whisperings of my soul said, *Re-open your heart to your husband though you're still angry. Re-open your heart to your husband though you're still hurt. Re-open your heart though he could mess up again. Re-open your heart—because you can choose to. Don't have it be dependent on his behavior or having to do something to earn it. Re-open your heart to your husband because you can.*

This was one of the most difficult things I've had to do in my life. Forgiveness started to soften my heart, and it enabled me to begin to recognize and own up to my parts of our problems. I had not taken full responsibility for my contribution to our marriage breakdown, nor done the self-forgiveness work for my own violation and betrayal in my marriage. I was able to take the energy of all the blame and anger that I was directing at my husband, and transform it from condemnation to liberation, blame to compassion, and guilt and shame to joy and love.

Congratulations on completing this portion of the journey!

Chapter Twenty

Growing Forward

Congratulations once again on completing the first 19 chapters of this book! The good news is that completing this book is only the beginning! Now the real fun begins as you continue your journey and grow forward.

S taying connected and continuing to build your Love Truth muscles are important next steps. This is not a quick "shot in the arm" kind of process, but one that is ongoing.

Developing and strengthening your new love relationships muscles is similar to building muscles in your physical body. First you provide a stimulus to the muscle, an action or condition that elicits a response. For example, with your physical body, lifting weights would be considered a stimulus. For your new love relationships muscles, the stimulus is engaging in the exercises associated with the Love Truths, putting into practice the detoxing actions and exercises that comprise the six steps of the B.L.I.S.S.S. Program, and knowing that the key is practice and not treating these actions and exercises as one-time events. After all, you don't get six-pack abs by doing one set of sit-ups. Your ab muscles develop and become pronounced over time as a "six-pack," as you strengthen them and burn the fat around them. The same principle applies here.

Second, when building muscles you must supply your body with the necessary nutrients. For your new love relationships muscles, this supply of nutrients can take the form of availing yourself of the ongoing offerings, free e-books, self-study courses, intensives and tele-courses on my websites (my other site is www.MillionDollarMentor.net); plugging into a Vitamin D meetup group, for example, or reading some of the books I've cited throughout this book.

Third in the muscle-building process is creating a suitable environ-ment for your ongoing work. This means doing what is necessary to sup-port yourself in integrating these new beliefs, thoughts, behaviors, and practices into your mind and then into your relationship(s). This includes being in the company of other women who also desire to be Relationships Revolutionaries, are serious about being in their woman, and who live the new relationships paradigm. This is one of the reasons I created the Vita-min D groups and also created book club questions—so that you could connect with like-minded women who are on a similar journey. (Vitamin D meet-up information is available through the www.DidYouBuyTheLove-Lies.com website.)

As we close out this leg of our journey together, let's do a recap of the first 10 Female Love Lies. Here's a "before and after" detox summary for you, that captures, on the left, some perspectives and concepts that you may have been operating from before you started reading this book, and then on the right, new perspectives and concepts born out of the Love Truths that I hope have begun to take root in your understanding and behavior after your detox process.

BEFORE detoxing from the Love Lies	AFTER detoxing from the Love Lies
Love is conditional.	Love is unconditional.
I'm looking for/trying to find a man.	I'm a living magnet.
I'm shopping for a man based upon a Requirements List.	I seek to embody the qualities I desire; I activate high-vibration qualities in a man.
A man must meet my needs and fulfill my expectations.	I co-create the experience I want to have, and I bring the mangoes!
I treat love as acquisition to be found, taken, forced, or "gotten" from another.	Love is experienced within and then shared from my fullness and overflow.
There is a sole soul mate.	Many soul mate possibilities exist.
I'm being "in my girl."	I'm being "in my woman."
I chase happiness.	I experience deep satisfaction and fulfillment.
I am defined by prescribed roles.	I am liberated by my divine assignments, functions, and gifts.
I make him responsible for my happiness.	I have an inner experience of joy and I share from the fullness of my spirit and the fruits of sacred self-care.
I idolize males/my husband.	I have appreciation of the male gifts; I praise and appreciate, not worship.

I date.	I am courted.
A man completes me.	I am already complete; I am the Gift.
I'm uni-lingual.	I'm bi-lingual.
I'm ineligible.	I'm eligible.
In covenant marriage, I believe that headship and leadership are one in the same.	I recognize that headship and leadership are distinct, separate, and complementary divine functions. The wife's feminine leadership and the husband's headship are different and are both essential to achieving and maintaining balance in a spiritual partnership; submitting and headship authority work together hand in hand.
In covenant marriage, I bought into a hierarchy of male superiority/female inferiority.	I understand that a man and woman are equal in personhood; have different and gifts; shared dominion; and a non-hierarchical divine partnership.
I am the follower.	I am the natural leader and the leader naturally (feminine leadership).
I believe self-love is optional.	I know that self-love is required.
I operate from scarcity.	I operate from abundance.
I am unhealed and have emotional baggage.	I am emotionally healed and free.
I can't change a man.	Oh, yes I can; a man is highly "seasonable."

Next Steps

The detoxing process returns you to your natural state—living in accord with the Love Truths instead of the Love Lies. In this natural state you are relaxed, confident, radiant, joyful, and able to give and receive graciously, you walk comfortably in your feminine power and essence. This is how the Love Truths gradually become the new norm—more and more women return to a natural and powerful way of relating. This is how you become a Relationship Revolutionary and this is how the revolution spreads.

As part of your new muscle-building support, I want to share the New Relationships Manifesto with you entitled, "I Say Yes!" As a manifesto it is your public declaration of intention. You can read, re-read, and share it. You can read it out loud, at the close of your Vitamin D gatherings, or at book club meetings. You'll see it on page 208.

A Way to Stay Engaged and Be Supported

I've created a way for women to connect and support one another in implementing and integrating the principles and practices introduced in this book. I call these Vitamin D gatherings. You might be interested in either starting a Vitamin D meet-up group or getting connected to one. A Vitamin D gathering is a group of five or more women, including yourself, who meet for the purpose of spirited dialogue and discussion about the principles and teachings in *The Love Lies*, and to actively support one another. A Vitamin D gathering can also serve as an accountability group for working through the detox process with other committed women.

For more information on Vitamin D meet-up groups, click on the Vitamin D link on the website. Also, arrangements can be made for me to call in to your gathering, via teleconference call, speakerphone, or video conferencing service if you have at least eight gathered. Please contact Info@DidYouBuytheLoveLies.com to make this request.

The website provides you support for your ongoing journey. It is designed to help you as you continue to condition your new love relationship muscles, and to support you in continually practicing and integrating the Love Truths into your relationships. The website is your source for information on the Love Academy, the full-day intensive from which the idea for this book was born, the Courtship Academy, Men-tality (for men only, half-day seminar), and tele-courses such as Woman Training, For Married Women Only, the 90-Day Radiance Plan, my free Pillow Talk Question & Answer forum, and a free e-book on Debrena's Courtship Principles.

Testimonies to share? I love to receive 'em! Please email your testimony to Info@DidYouBuyTheLoveLies.com. I may even use your testimony (anonymously) in future promotions. If you don't want to have your testimony anonymously used, please note this in your email.

The Masterminds/Love Academy Offices: 206-878-8163

Email: To reach me about a speaking engagement or the criteria for bringing the Love Academy or one of my live events to your city, please go to the website and click on the Love Academy tab for details and send your email to Info@DidYouBuyTheLoveLies.com

Twitter: @TheDVine#TheLoveLies

About the Author

Debrena Jackson Gandy has been featured in magazines such as Oprah's *O, Essence, Woman's Day, Ebony, Empowering Women, Black Enterprise,* and *Heart & Soul* as well as on Oprah.com. She is a success coach and love relationships mentor to hundreds; direct-selling speaker and trainer; founder of the Love Academy; creator of five e-books, a self-published book on direct-selling/multi-level marketing success (an award-winning leader of a direct-selling team of nearly 3,000 women), and a plethora of transformational courses, retreats, tele-courses, and tele-seminars. She's been a popular guest on more than 40 radio shows, and has been seen on CNN, *CNN Live, Good Day New York, Good Morning Texas,* C-SPAN, *In Style,* the Wisdom Channel, Fox 5 Morning News, and several ABC News affiliates and regional news stations. She is also one of the TV show hosts of *Public Report* on TBN's station KTBW Seattle/Tacoma.

Debrena is a keynote speaker, business consultant and trainer to large and small businesses, universities, entrepreneurs, multilevel marketing and direct-selling companies and field leaders.

She resides in Seattle, Washington. She and her husband have three beautiful, brilliant daughters, and have been married 21 years and counting. . . .

You can reach Debrena on Twitter through @TheDVine.

The New Relationships Manifesto
I Say Yes!

I say Yes to being a Relationships Revolutionary
I say Yes to being part of a movement to
elevate how women and men engage and relate
I say Yes to letting go of false beliefs
and toxic thinking and behavior
I say Yes to forgiveness and freeing my mind,
body, spirit, and womb of emotional baggage
I say Yes to boldly and courageously
breaking the shackles of the Love Lies off of my
mind, body, and spirit
I say Yes to the divine self-work
that is a necessary part of my detox process
I choose to open my heart
I say Yes to sacred self-care
I embrace being The Gift
I celebrate my awakening into Woman
I say Yes to new possibilities for love
I Say Yes! I Say Yes! I SAY YES!

© 2014 Debrena Jackson Gandy

Bibliography

Afua, Queen. *Sacred Woman*. New York, NY: Ballantine Publishing Group, 2000.

Baines, John. *The Science of Love*. New York, NY: The Dario Salas Institute for Hermetic Science, 1988.

Bloomfield, Harold and Kory, Robert B. Kory. *Inner Joy*. New York: Wyden Books, 1980.

Brown, Jr., Victor. *Human Intimacy*. Salt Lake City, UT: Parliament Publishers, 1981.

Carter, Jimmy. *A Call to Action: Women, Religion, Violence and Power*. New York: Simon & Schuster, 2014.

Deida, David. *Intimate Communion*. Deerfield Beach, FL: Health Communications, Inc., 1995.

"Divorce Rate Statistics—Countries Compared." NationMaster.
    Accessed September 27, 2013. www.nationmaster/graph/peop_div_rat-people-divorce-rate.

"Does Living Together Before Marriage Increase Chances of Divorce?"
    eHarmony Blog. Accessed December 14, 2013.
    www.eharmony.com/blog/2013/07/24/
    does-living-together-before-marriage-increase-chances-of-divorce.

Foundation for Inner Peace. *A Course in Miracles*. Glen Ellen, CA: Foundation for Inner Peace Publishing, 1975.

Gattuso, Joan. *A Course in Love*. San Francisco, CA: HarperCollins Publishers, 1996.

Greenberg, Melanie. "The Mindful Self-Express: Ten Science-Based Facts About Love." Accessed November 20, 2013. www.psychologytoday.com/blog/the-mindful-self-express.

Hay, Louise. *You Can Heal Your Life*. Carlsbad, CA: Hay House, 1999.

"Hofstede Individualism Trait." Accessed November 22, 2013.
    www.andrews.edu/~tidwell/bsad560/HofsteveIndividualism.html.

Holy Bible, *The Woman's Study Bible*, New King James Version. New York: Thomas Nelson Publishers, 2009.

Jackson Gandy, Debrena. *All the Joy You Can Stand*. New York, NY: Random House, 2000.

———. *Sacred Pampering Principles*. New York, NY: William Morrow & Company, a division of HarperCollins Publishers, 1997.

McWilliams, Peter. *Love 101*. Los Angeles, CA: Prelude Press, 1995.

Moschetta, Evelyn and Paul. *The Marriage Spirit*. New York: Simon & Schuster, 1998.

"Non-U.S. Divorce Rates—Divorce Statistics Collection." Accessed September 27, 2013. www.divorcereform.org/nonus.html#anchor5599108.

Northup, Christiane. *Women's Bodies, Women's Wisdom*. New York: Bantam Books, 1994.

Osho. *Love, Freedom, Aloneness*. New York, NY: St. Martin's Griffin, 2001.

Page, Ken. "Recognizing Your Attractions of Deprivation." *Psychology Today*. Accessed December 21, 2013. www.psychologytoday.com/blog/findings-love.

Paxman, Rosemary. "Egg Cells Send Out Chemical Signals to Entice Sperm." *BioNews.org.uk*
    Accessed December 12, 2013. www.bionews.org.uk/page_91379.asp.

Pope, David and Barbara Dafoe Whitehead. *"The State of Our Unions 2010."* The National Marriage Project. Charlottesville, VA: University of Virginia Press, 2009.

———. *The State of Our Unions 2013*. The National Marriage Project. Charlottesville, VA: University of Virginia Press, 2012.

Price, Eugenia. *Woman to Woman*. New York, NY: Zondervan Publishing, a division of HarperCollins Publishers, 1959.

Reilly, Patricia Lynn. *Imagine a Woman in Love with Herself*. Berkeley, CA: Conari Press, 1999.

"Romance Through the Ages—History of Romance & Dating Customs." Accessed November 26, 2013. www.genealogy.com/cs/timelines/a/romance_history.htm.

Scott, Stuart. *The Exemplary Husband*. Bemidji, MN: Focus Publishing, 2002.

"Study Examines Potential Evolutionary Role of 'Sexual Regret' in Human Survival and Reproduction." Accessed November 25, 2013. www.utexas.edu/news/human-survival-and-reproduction.html.

Tannen, Deborah. *That's Not What I Meant!* New York, NY: Ballantine Publishing Group, A Division of Random House, Inc., 1986

"The Differences Between Eastern and Western Philosophy." Accessed November 22, 2013. www.thinkaboutit-knowaboutit.com/2013/04/the-difference-between-Eastern-and-Western-Philosophy.html.

"The Four Kinds of Authority—Gordon Training International." Accessed December 31, 2013. www.gordontraining.com/free-parenting-articles/the-four-kinds-of-authority.html.

"The Process of Muscle Growth—Quick Muscle Building Tips." Accessed December 8, 2013. www.quick-muscle-building-tips.com/the-process-of-muscle-growth.html.

"The Relationship Between Divorce Rates and Individualism vs. Collectivism." Accessed September 27, 2013. www.mrhanson.weebly.com/albeekim-divorce-and-individualism-collectivism.html.

Vitale, Joe. Zero Limits: The Secret Hawaiian System for Wealth, Health, Peace & More. Hoboken, New Jersey: John Wiley & Sons, 2007.

"Women's Reproductive Health: Hysterectomy Fact Sheet." Accessed December 20, 2013. www.cdc.gov/reproductivehealth/womensrh.html.

Index